THE BOARD-SAVVY CEO:

Building a High-Impact Partnership With Your Board

By
Doug Eadie
President & CEO
Doug Eadie & Company, Inc.

A Governance Edge™ Publication

A publication of
Governance Edge™
Doug Eadie & Company
3 Sunny Point Terrace
Oldsmar, FL 34677

Phone: 800.209.7652
E-mail: Doug@DougEadie.com
A complete listing of books by Doug Eadie is available at
www.DougEadie.com.

ISBN 978-0-9798894-9-3

Library of Congress Control Number: 2013955690

Library of Congress Subject Headings:
Nonprofit organizations
Boards of directors

Cover and interior design by Van-garde Imagery

For Barbara, Jennifer, and William
and in Memory of
Lena and William Eadie and
Fannie and Charles Crawford

TABLE OF CONTENTS

FOREWORD

My years of experience as both a nonprofit board member and foundation executive have taught me that extraordinary governance is critical to the long-term success of nonprofit and public organizations, in terms of realizing their vision and carrying out their mission. I've also learned from long experience that the nonprofit and public boards that do the kind of high-impact governing these challenging times demand work in close partnership with a chief executive officer who is what author Doug Eadie calls "board savvy." Sad to say, many CEOs I've observed over the years haven't been board savvy enough to build the kind of close, positive, and productive partnership with their board that is at the heart of high-impact governing, which is why I'm delighted that Doug Eadie has written *The Board-Savvy CEO*.

A powerful addition to the nonprofit/public governance literature, *The Board-Savvy CEO* is a rich resource for nonprofit and public board members, CEOs, and CEO-aspirants. Drawing on his twenty-five years of work with hundreds of nonprofit and public organizations, Doug Eadie's newest book provides the reader with a treasure trove of detailed, practical, and thoroughly tested guidance for mastering the three key roles of the board-savvy CEO:

- taking the lead in developing the board's capacity to do the kind of high-impact governing work that makes a real difference in an organization's affairs;

- helping the board to map out processes for actively engaging board members and transforming them into strong *owners* of their governing decisions and judgments; and

- working closely with the board to ensure that the board-CEO working relationship is healthy enough to withstand the inevitable pressures that every organization experiences in this rapidly changing world.

One of the many gems you will find in *The Board-Savvy CEO* is Doug's fresh look at the detailed work of governing. What boards do when they govern, according to Doug, is make a never-ending stream of judgments and decisions that determine where an organization is headed over the long run, what the organization is now and in the near term, and how the organization is performing. Doug's dynamic view of governing work couldn't be more different from the conventional and static notion of governing as mere "policy making."

If you are deeply concerned about the leadership of nonprofit and public organizations of all shapes and sizes, you will want to add *The Board-Savvy CEO* to your reading — and rereading — list and keep it close at hand as a powerful leadership resource.

Robert E. Eckardt
Executive Vice President
The Cleveland Foundation

ACKNOWLEDGMENTS

I am indebted to the hundreds of nonprofit and public board members, chief executive officers, and senior managers I've worked with over the past twenty-five years. The practical guidance you will find in the following pages draws heavily on the lessons I've learned from my hands-on consulting work with them, helping to develop their boards' governing capacity and to build strong board-chief executive partnerships.

This book has benefited tremendously from the input of thirty-plus nonprofit and public leaders who participated in a series of teleconferences, during which they commented on the book's key concepts and structure. Deserving my heartfelt thanks are: Abe Abraham, President/CEO, CMI Management, Inc.; Audrey Alvarado, former Vice President, Nonprofit Roundtable of Greater Washington; Carm Basile, Chief Executive Officer, Capital District Transportation Authority; David Baumgardner, President and CEO, LifeNet, Inc.; Robert Betz, PhD, President, American Association of Eye and Ear Centers of Excellence; Stephen G. Bland, former Chief Executive Officer, Port Authority of Allegheny County; Eileen Coogan Boyle, President and CEO, Allegany Franciscan Ministries; Richard Browdie, President and CEO, Benjamin Rose Institute on Aging; Ronnie Bryant, CEcD, FM, President and CEO, Charlotte Regional Partnership; Sue Buchholtz, President and CEO, Evergreen Life Services; Joseph A. Calabrese, Chief Executive Officer, Greater Cleveland Regional Transit Authority; Gary Conley, President, TechSolve, Inc.; Ken A. Crerar, President/CEO, Council of Insurance Agents and Brokers; Robert E. Eckardt, Executive Vice President, The Cleveland Foundation; Melissa Fahy, Chief Executive Officer, Good Samaritan Health Clinic of Pasco, Inc.; Jeff Finkle, President/CEO, International Economic Development

Council; Kurt Foreman, Executive Vice President — Economic Development, Oklahoma City Chamber of Commerce; Christopher H. Fox, Executive Director, International and American Associations for Dental Research; Lynne Thomas Gordon, CAE, FACHE, Chief Executive Officer, American Health Information Management Association; Karen Higgins, President and CEO, PARC; Wendy W. Kavanagh, CAE, President, Georgia Society of Association Executives; Charles Macfarlane, FACHE, CAE, Chief Executive Officer, American Association of Diabetes Educators; Gregory Maciag, President and CEO, ACORD; James McGuirk, PhD, Executive Director/CEO, Astor Services for Children & Families; Michael Melaniphy, President and CEO, American Public Transportation Association; Susan Meyer, Chief Executive Officer, Spokane Transit; Joel Ratner, President and CEO, Neighborhood Progress, Inc.; Stuart Rogel, President and CEO, Tampa Bay Partnership; Cheryl Ronk, CAE, CMP, President, Michigan Society of Association Executives; Jeffrey Shields, FASAE, CAE, President and CEO, National Business Officers Association; Jeannette Stawski, CAE, Executive Director, Association of Outdoor Recreation and Education; Christie Tarantino, FASAE, CAE, President and CEO, Association Forum of Chicagoland; Jim Thompson, CAE, IOM, Executive Director, Association Executives of North Carolina; Kathleen Van De Loo, Founding President, Association Development Group, Inc.; Lana Vukovljak, Chief Executive Officer, Council of Residential Specialists.

Over the years, I have been afforded the opportunity to explore concepts that are at the heart of this book in major professional publications, and I would accordingly like to thank: Julie Shoop, Vice President/Editor-in-Chief, *Associations Now* (American Society of Association Executives); Heather Ryndak Swink, Executive Editor, *Forum* (Association Forum of Chicagoland); Dr. Norman A. Dolch, Editor-in-Chief, *Journal of Nonprofit Education and Leadership*; and Jill Muehrcke, Editor, *Nonprofit World* (Society for Nonprofits).

During my visit to the great city of Cleveland, Ohio, last April —
primarily to join my son, William, and his lovely wife, Christine, in
celebrating the baptism of their daughter, Stella Elinor — I was fortunate to spend an hour with Robert Eckardt, Executive Vice President
of the Cleveland Foundation and the author of the Foreword to this
book. Sitting in Bob's office six months ago, I recalled the important
role this distinguished philanthropic institution had played in the development of my career as a nonprofit consultant. The Foundation's
funding my work with several of Cleveland's neighborhood development corporations, including Slavic Village Development and the St.
Clair-Superior Development Corporation, early in my career cemented
my commitment to capacity building in the nonprofit sector. It gives
me great pleasure, at last, to acknowledge my debt to the Foundation,
which is one of Cleveland's — and the nation's — precious assets.

I've acknowledged the invaluable lessons I've learned from the
hundreds of board members and CEOs I've worked with over the
years, which have made this book a far more powerful resource for
nonprofit and public leaders. In this regard, I must single out my
long-standing professional and personal relationship with Jeff Finkle, President and CEO of the International Economic Development
Council. Not only did Jeff and I work closely together in developing
the governing capacity of the Board of Directors of IEDC not long
after the merger creating this international economic development
powerhouse, Jeff has also provided me with numerous opportunities
over the past twenty years to present workshops and web seminars
for IEDC members, whose feedback has been critical in honing many
of the key concepts in this book. I am pleased to acknowledge Jeff's
contribution to my professional success and to thank him, as well, for
the friendship that has enriched our association.

Tom Berger, President of Orange Street Editorial, deserves my
heartfelt appreciation for very capably handling the myriad details in-

volved in transforming this manuscript into a published work, as he has for the four other books I've written for Governance Edge. I have come to rely on Tom's keen editorial eye and meticulous attention to detail, which have made my work as a writer much more productive and far less stressful than it otherwise might be.

As always, this book has benefited from the insightful suggestions of my two children, Jenny and William, and of my sister and dear friend Kay Sue Nagle. I well know that if something I've written doesn't pass muster with Jenny, William and Kay Sue, it absolutely must not appear in print, so I always take their suggestions for improvement very, very seriously. And I am always deeply touched by their willingness to take time from extremely demanding careers to advise me, expecting only my love as compensation. Thank you once again, Jenny, William, and Kay Sue!

Finally, I must acknowledge the contribution of my wife and closest friend, Barbara Carlson Krai. Her steadfast love and support provide the essential emotional foundation for my creative labor as a writer, and her always thoughtful advice on critical issues has made every book I've written during our marriage much better than it otherwise would have been. A solid marriage is truly a blessing in many more ways than one! Thank you, Barbara.

Of course, I am solely responsible for whatever flaws the reader might find in this book.

Doug Eadie
Tampa Bay, Florida
October 10, 2013

CHAPTER ONE

THE BOARD-SAVVY CEO IN A NUTSHELL

HIGH STAKES — BIG PAYOFF

The Board-Savvy CEO is a "survive-and-thrive" handbook for nonprofit chief executive officers (CEOs) and executives aspiring to become CEOs somewhere down the road. My aim is to provide the CEOs and CEO-aspirants reading this book with detailed, practical, thoroughly tested guidance that they can add to their CEO tool kit and put to immediate use in raising their governing IQ and becoming more board savvy. I've written this book not only for CEOs who are new to the job, but also for seasoned CEOs who — in the spirit of continuous improvement — want to beef up their board savviness in order to maintain a really solid working relationship with their boards, as experienced board members rotate off their governing bodies, new, less experienced members join their boards, and emerging issues claim board and CEO attention. Nonprofit board members who are committed to working in close partnership with their CEO in getting the tremendously important work of governing accomplished will also find this book a useful resource in partnership building and in making sure that the next CEO they recruit is sufficiently board savvy to be an effective partner with their board.

"Survive and thrive" might sound like a bit of hyperbole, but my twenty-five years of work with hundreds of nonprofit boards and CEOs have taught me that the stakes involved in a CEO's strengthening his governing IQ — in becoming more board savvy — are tremendously high. The CEO's career as well as the long-run success of the nonprofit she works for heavily depend on the CEO's investment in growing her board savviness. In the first place, although it won't sound very altruistic, I've learned from experience that board-savvy CEOs tend not only to last longer in the CEO position than their less board-savvy CEO colleagues but also to achieve their executive leadership goals more fully, primarily because they're more adept at building and maintaining close, positive, and productive partnerships with their boards that can withstand the inevitable stresses and strains at the top of the organization, where boards and CEOs do their work. Board-savvy CEOs, then, tend to survive longer in a profession where turnover has been accelerating for years. Such stability, as any nonprofit leader who has gone through an expensive, time-consuming CEO recruitment process knows, is a tremendous organizational asset.

But the stakes involve more than a CEO's lengthened tenure and enhanced executive leadership. More altruistically, I've learned over the years that nonprofit organizations whose CEOs are board savvy tend to thrive in this rapidly changing, challenging world. Over the long run, they do a better job of translating their long-range visions into practice, carrying out their missions fully, and achieving organizational stability, innovation, and growth. The reason is simple. Their boards, working in close partnership with a board-savvy CEO, do a consistently good job of doing what I think of as "high-impact" governing: regularly and systematically making the kinds of high-stakes governing judgments and decisions that make an important difference in the affairs of their nonprofits.

A BRIEF LOOK AT THE CEO POSITION

The term *CEO* appears over and over in this book, so I'd like to take a minute to define it before moving on. Whatever the working title your nonprofit employs — *executive director, chief executive officer, president and CEO, superintendent* (public school districts), or *general manager* (transportation authorities) — your nonprofit's CEO is almost without exception the highest-ranking, paid professional staff member who is hired by and accountable to the board and who is responsible for directing all internal operations. Many CEOs play a major role in external relations as well, serving as the public spokesperson of their nonprofit in the media and speaking on behalf of their nonprofit in such forums as the chamber of commerce and Rotary Club locally and association annual meetings at the state and national level. This external relations role is almost always shared with the board chair, and increasingly, in my experience, with other board members. Keep in mind that the CEO is never a volunteer, unless the nonprofit she serves is totally volunteer driven, having no paid staff at all. The CEO is virtually never a voting member of the board; however, there is a growing trend to make CEOs nonvoting board members, which I think is an excellent step.

SOME BOARD-SAVVY CEOs AT WORK

Let me tell you about some recent examples of board-savvy CEOs who have partnered with their boards to produce impressive results in a challenging environment. There's Carm Basile, who worked closely with his board at the Capital District Transportation Authority in Albany, New York, which provides bus service in the four-county Albany region, to significantly reduce the agency's administrative costs to bring them into alignment with revenues, while managing at the same time to significantly grow ridership. David Baumgardner partnered with his board at LifeNet, Inc., which provides emergency medical transportation, in expanding the geographical reach — and consequently the financial resources and organizational clout — of his Texarkana, Texas-based nonprofit, which continues to expand aggressively. Richard Browdie provided strong support and guidance to the board of Cleveland's Benjamin Rose Institute on Aging in making the courageous strategic decision to exit the nursing home business and to concentrate on other facets of this prestigious nonprofit's mission. Sue Buchholtz worked closely with her board at Evergreen Life Services, a nonprofit serving individuals with developmental disabilities based in Haughton, Louisiana, to get this six-state organization involved in highly innovative income-generating social enterprises as an important means of diversifying its revenues and also providing productive work and learning experiences for its clients. Jeff Finkle intensively involved members of two large boards to accomplish the merger of two increasingly competitive national economic development associations — the American Economic Development Council and the Council for Urban Economic Development — thereby creating the International Economic Development Council and later worked closely with his new board to make IEDC an international powerhouse in the field of economic development.

Christopher Fox partnered with the boards of the International and American Associations for Dental Research, headquartered in the Washington, DC, area, in accomplishing a major restructuring of both boards that has resulted not only in higher-impact governing decisions and significantly stronger board member engagement but has also put in place a critical piece of the foundation for future growth worldwide. Virginia Jacko at the Miami Lighthouse for the Blind worked closely with her board to accomplish a strategic merger that created the Heiken Children's Vision Program, expanding the Lighthouse mission to include providing eye exams for underserved children. Susan Meyer, with the strong support of her board at the Spokane Transit Authority, committed $1 million to STA's innovative Quality Counts Initiative, including the Mystery Shopper Program, which took customer service to the next level. There's Pam Shea, who as superintendent of schools, collaborated with the board of the Teton County School District #1 in producing a succinct, powerful strategic plan for this Jackson Hole, Wyoming, district that ensures a bright future for this outstanding educational enterprise, in terms of growing student achievement, increased organizational stability, and wider community understanding and support. And there's Lana Vukovljak, who partnered with the board of the American Association of Diabetes Educators in implementing a far-reaching redesign of their member involvement structure that has tremendously strengthened volunteerism in the association while redeploying resources that had been consumed in supporting the traditional chapter model.

These are just a few of the many outstanding, truly board-savvy CEOs I've worked with, whose experiences have demonstrated the critical importance of a CEO's being board savvy and have provided me with a powerful incentive to write *The Board-Savvy CEO*.

OTHER SURE SIGNS OF A BOARD-SAVVY CEO AT WORK

I've pointed out two preeminent signs that there's a board-savvy CEO at work in a nonprofit organization. First, the nonprofit thrives and grows over the long run, primarily because the board works closely with its CEO in doing a solid job of making high-stakes governing decisions and judgments that capitalize on growth opportunities and counter threats in a rapidly changing, always challenging environment. Second, the CEO not only provides outstanding executive leadership but also has more staying power in a tremendously difficult job. Let's take a look at three other sure signs that indicate there's a board-savvy CEO at work in the nonprofit. For one thing, board members find their governing work deeply satisfying — definitely worth all the time and effort they're dedicating to governing — and they feel like owners of the important governing judgments and decisions they make. Second, board members tend not to get involved in nongoverning administrative work; in other words, you won't find them doing what we call "micromanaging." And, third, the board-CEO partnership is rock-solid — able to withstand the inevitable stresses and strains at the top of every nonprofit.

SATISFIED OWNERS OF THEIR GOVERNING WORK

Over the years, wearing my nonprofit consulting hat, I've interviewed hundreds of board members in the process of preparing for board retreats and strategic-planning work sessions. I always ask: "Tell me about your experience as a board member. What's it been like being part of this board?" If I hear answers like the ones from board members of a health clinic I worked with recently that serves low-income, uninsured clients, I can be pretty sure there's a CEO at work who has a lot of board savviness. "I feel like I'm making a tremendous difference in the community, and I'm learning a lot to boot." "I can't tell you how much it means to me that we're doing a top-notch job of meeting a really pressing need." "Working on this board is challenging, but worth the time and effort." "Committee and board meetings are tremendously productive, and I feel like my time is well spent."

The board members of this clinic weren't only satisfied with their governing experience, they also felt like owners of their governing work, and I've learned over the years that nonprofit board member satisfaction and feelings of ownership are two of the linchpins of a rock-solid board-CEO partnership. Satisfaction comes — above all else — from board members being actively engaged in doing important governing work that capitalizes on the abundant resources that they bring to the boardroom — their knowledge, expertise, experience, connections with key stakeholders, money, and even more — and that impacts the affairs of their nonprofit in major ways. In other words, they're intensively involved in making a real difference. Board member satisfaction also comes from involvement in governing work that is interesting, ego satisfying, and even now and then fun.

Closely related to satisfaction is ownership, one of the most powerful forces at work in leadership and the preeminent source of board member loyalty and commitment. In a nutshell, board members' feelings of ownership result from their meaningful involvement early enough in making governing decisions to shape those decisions in significant ways. For example, Pam Shea's school board out in Jackson Hole, Wyoming, was involved intensively — from the get-go — in the planning process that resulted in the Teton County School District's updated strategic plan, so by the time Pam's board members formally adopted the plan, this major governing product truly belonged to them. If Pam hadn't been so board savvy, she might have taken a more traditional and straightforward approach: merely having staff and/or a consultant just go ahead and crank out a strategic planning document and sending the finished plan to the board to thumb through and comment on. The board might have been an appreciative audience for the plan, admiring its logic and relevance, but they wouldn't have been committed owners who could be counted on to support the plan over the long haul.

I wish I could report that the majority of board members I've encountered over the years have been satisfied owners of their governing work, but, sad to say, the overwhelming majority, based on my interviews, have felt unfulfilled, underutilized, disengaged, dissatisfied, frustrated, disappointed, and the like. For example, when I interviewed the board members of a large national professional association a few months ago, responses to my question about the governing experience were typical of what I hear much of the time: "We spend all our time just listening to staff reports in board meetings — boring!" "I'm really not sure what my role is, and I definitely don't feel like I'm making much of a difference." "We just thumbed through the finished line-item budget a month before we had to vote on it, so any changes we could make at that point were pretty trivial — really a waste of our time." "I can't say we're making any really strategic decisions or dealing with any of our high-stakes issues; it's like, you know, Nero fiddling while Rome was burning."

Early in my consulting career, the pressing need for a board-savvy CEO to concentrate on building feelings of satisfaction and ownership among board members was vividly brought home, teaching me a lesson I fortunately took to heart and incorporated into my consulting tool kit. I was working with one of the smartest, technically most capable CEOs I've ever met. He actually intimidated me on occasion, which was no mean feat. He — let's call him "Howard" — was in many ways an executive virtuoso, who'd really mastered his leadership craft — with one notable exception that proved deadly. Early one morning, walking into Howard's office to discuss the upcoming board meeting, I found him ashen faced. "For heaven's sake, Howard," I said, "what's happened?" "Here," he replied, handing me a piece of paper, "read this and tell me what you think." It turned out to be the board's most recent evaluation of Howard's chief executive performance. As I worked my way down the page, I couldn't figure out what the problem was; Howard was scoring really high on every item that had been ranked: strategic planning, financial management, public relations, and the like. But when I got to the bottom, I found that the board had decided he should ply his CEO trade elsewhere. In effect, what they said was, "You're really great at what you do, but you've left us out of the action. We feel uninvolved, uncreative, and condescended to. We've had it, and you're out."

If feelings of deep board member satisfaction and ownership — these linchpins of solid board-CEO partnerships — were routine spin-offs of nonprofit board work, my hundreds of interviews would have resulted in a radically different database. What I've learned is that it takes lots of good thinking, planning and nuts-and-bolts process design to generate the kind of meaningful, active board member involvement that fosters satisfaction and ownership, and only a board-savvy CEO has the knowledge and time to get the job done. The boards of the International and American Associations for Dental Research couldn't — on their own — have designed and carried out the process that resulted in their becoming strong owners of a new board structure. They would have failed not because they weren't smart or dedicated enough, but because only their board-savvy CEO, Christopher Fox, had the time and expertise to figure out the steps involved (such as retaining a governance consultant to help plan and facilitate a daylong retreat that would involve them intensively at the very onset of the restructuring process) and to get the process implemented fully and on time.

MICROMANAGING NOTABLE BY ITS ABSENCE

The specter of board members getting involved in the nitty-gritty of pure managerial work, thereby encroaching on executive prerogatives and probably making a real mess of things they're not qualified to handle, worries more than a few CEOs. When I'm presenting keynotes

and workshops on building strong, enduring board-CEO partnerships, I repeatedly hear questions like this: "OK, Doug, you make a
pretty convincing case that we've got to involve our boards early and
intensively in shaping key governing decisions as the preeminent way
of turning them into real owners of their governing work. And I can
see how involving my board members in well-designed structure (like
a board planning committee) and processes (like annual budget preparation) can foster this kind of involvement. But aren't we potentially
opening Pandora's box by inviting this level of engagement?" My response is always the same: "Absolutely not!" In fact, the opposite is
true. Intensive, early, meaningful board involvement in key governing
processes is the surest safeguard against micromanaging because the
board is so busy doing serious governing work that it doesn't have
either the time or motivation to dabble in nongoverning work.

The good news, as long experience has taught me, is that the great
majority of board members arrive at the boardroom with the best of
intentions. They sincerely want to make a positive difference. They
want to do a really great job of governing. They aren't the least bit interested in dabbling in nongoverning administrative work. Of course,
there are always a few bad apples in the barrel — like the new board
member I encountered recently who was hell-bent on pursuing a narrow, single-item agenda: radically trimming down such "luxuries" as
staff conference attendance — but I've learned that they're the rare
exception to the rule. Here's the rub — a real double whammy. In the
first place, the typically high-achieving, bright, ambitious, busy board
member passionately wanting to make a difference very often doesn't
know much about the nuts-and-bolts work of governing, nor does
she have the time to become a world-class governance expert. And
worse, a CEO without much board savviness has all too often failed
to develop structure and processes to engage board members proac-

tively — early enough to have significant impact — in doing serious governing work. The classic example is a CEO who sends her board a finished budget document, asking only that board members thumb through it and ask any questions they might have about one item or another. Board members, in lieu of any serious work to do, will naturally dig into the minor details, being major-league doers who can't stand being passive. They fill vacuums — naturally, aggressively — and if this means micromanagement, so be it. Anything is better than standing around twiddling their thumbs.

CEOs who aren't very board savvy sometimes think they can avert board micromanagement by fashioning a set of policies defining the rules (often called "policies") well-behaved board members should follow (such as focusing on "ends" rather than "means"). But in lieu of serious board member engagement, a set of rules is worse than useless; it actually builds an appetite for micromanagement because of the vacuum resulting from the absence of board engagement. Around five years ago, I got a call from a CEO asking me if I'd spend an hour with him and his board chair on the telephone, discussing a real dilemma they'd gotten into. When we finally got together telephonically a week later, it turned out that the board of this large international professional association was immersed in administrative details, extremely frustrated, and on the verge of revolt. The CEO's job was without question in jeopardy. It was a classic case that I've seen more than once. Board members had worked for several months with a consultant to develop an elaborate policy manual that at great length distinguished between board and CEO authority and functions, providing clear-cut rules of the game at the top. However, no attention had been paid to engaging board members proactively and creatively in key processes like annual operational planning, in ways that would turn them into owners. It was like handing soccer players a rulebook and expecting that they'd be able to play the game. The inevitable upshot: board members feeling disengaged and not seeing any practical way to become engaged had gotten involved in myriad nongoverning activities — a classic case of idle hands doing you know whose work. Board-savvy CEOs, being keenly aware of the danger that underutilized, underinvolved board members will micromanage, wouldn't let this kind of preventable situation develop.

A ROCK-SOLID BOARD-CEO PARTNERSHIP WITH REAL STAYING POWER

One of the most important ways for me to assess the board savviness of a CEO is to ask his board members during the interview process kicking off a consulting engagement to assess their board's working relationship with the CEO by answering questions like these: How productive is it? Do you work harmoniously together? What relationship issues are causing tension? How are you dealing with them? What would you do to improve the working relationship? When the responses are pretty uniformly positive, I can be pretty certain that I'll be working with a truly board-savvy CEO, because the sad fact is that board-CEO partnerships are difficult to build and maintain, and they can erode alarmingly quickly, exacting a steep price in terms of reduced governing effectiveness, a tarnished organizational image, and diminished organizational clout. Since no board I am aware of over the long course of human history has ever fired itself for lackluster governing performance or for an eroded relationship with its chief executive, the CEO is almost always the victim of a failed partnership.

I'll never forget the dismal spectacle of all-too-public board-CEO bickering at a public transportation authority of a major city where I lived a few years ago. The CEO was eventually — painfully and brutally — ousted, but well before his exit, the authority had suffered massive loss of public confidence and support, key initiatives such as a new express bus line were jettisoned, and staff morale had plummeted. Two things struck me at the time: how quickly the board-CEO working relationship had come unraveled and the fact that the downward spiral of the relationship was occurring at a point when the transportation authority wasn't going through anything close to an operational crisis — ridership was holding steady, finances were in pretty good shape, and the operation was running pretty efficiently.

Even under the best of circumstances, board-CEO partnerships by their very nature are fragile and prone to rapid deterioration. This shouldn't come as any surprise when you think about it. After all, we're talking about a potentially volatile mix of strong-willed, ambitious board members and CEOs who are grappling with complex, high-stakes issues in a rapidly changing and always challenging world. The stresses and strains involved in leadership at the top can wear out a board-CEO working relationship alarmingly quickly, and having a board-savvy CEO at the executive helm is probably the most important factor in beating the odds and maintaining a really close, productive, and enduring partnership. What a truly board-savvy CEO well knows is that, no matter how important, it's not enough to make sure board members are intensively — and proactively — involved in doing meaningful governing work, making decisions and judgments that really do make an important difference. The board-savvy CEO is keenly aware that she must spend a lot of time focusing on the nuts-and-bolts details of plain old relationship management, having to do with such things as formal and informal communication, interaction guidelines, and the identification and resolution of relationship issues.

THREE KEY ROLES OF THE BOARD-SAVVY CEO

The following three chapters take a close look at three really critical roles that board-savvy CEOs play as they go about building rock-solid partnerships with their boards that result in high-impact governing decisions and judgments. My counsel in the following three chapters isn't theoretically exotic or technically very complex. For the most part, it's just good old common sense that's been successfully applied by many board-savvy CEOs in real-life nonprofit settings. Fortunately, in describing the three key roles that board-savvy CEOs play, I have been able to draw on the real-life experience of many CEOs all over the country who have successfully put their board savviness to work in the interest of high-impact governing and solid working relationships with their boards.

Chapter Two: The Board-Savvy CEO as Chief Board Capacity Builder

Board-savvy CEOs must take the lead in developing their boards' governing capacity, wearing the Chief Board Capacity Builder hat, because board members, being part-time volunteers, have neither the knowledge nor the time to spearhead board development. The board-savvy CEO is also keenly aware of the danger of ill-conceived, board-driven governance reform that is likely to cause more harm than good, such as employing bylaws revision as a major capacity-building tool or sliding down the slippery slope of board downsizing, consequently weakening the board as a governing resource by reducing its collective experience, expertise, knowledge, skills, external connections, and clout.

As the Chief Board Capacity Builder, the board-savvy CEO builds board members' appetite for systematically strengthening their governing capacity, rather than merely inheriting the board of today or yesterday; when called for, assists the board in designing and carrying out systematic board development initiatives aimed at large-scale change, such as a redefined board role, a new structure of board standing committees, and significantly strengthened processes for managing board performance; and when a contemporary, well-designed board committee structure is in place, helps the board use its standing committees as continuous governance improvement vehicles that generate incremental governance improvements year to year.

Chapter Three: The Board-Savvy CEO as Chief Governing Process Designer

The board-savvy CEO is keenly aware that board members make for more positive and productive governing partners when they are satisfied owners of their governing work and that playing a leading role in designing the board's governing processes is the preeminent means of generating satisfaction and ownership. Wearing the Chief Governing Process Designer hat, the board-savvy CEO takes the lead in designing practical ways to engage board members in key governing processes such as planning, performance monitoring, and external relations so as to strengthen both satisfaction and ownership; recommends additional ways to expand board member ownership, for example by regularly rotating standing committee chairs; ensures that board members are provided ample opportunity for ego satisfaction, through such means as making reports at full board meetings; and looks for opportunities to make the governing experience more interesting and enjoyable.

Chapter Four: The Board-Savvy CEO as Chief Governing Relationship Manager

Recognizing that the board-CEO working relationship is in the best of times fragile and always prone to deteriorate rapidly, the board-savvy CEO takes the lead in meticulously managing the relationship. Wearing the Chief Governing Relationship Manager hat, the board-savvy CEO works closely with the board committee responsible for maintaining the board-CEO partnership; reaches agreement with this committee on formal guidelines for CEO interaction and communication with the board as a whole and with individual board members and on the guidelines to govern board communication and interaction with staff who report to the CEO; places a high priority on developing a close working relationship with the board chair; reaches agreement with the board on her "CEO-centric" executive leadership targets; and makes sure that an effective process for board evaluation of CEO performance is designed and carried out at least annually.

BEING PREPARED TO PLAY THESE ROLES SUCCESSFULLY

The board-savvy CEOs I've observed who have been highly successful at playing the roles of Chief Board Capacity Builder, Chief Governing Process Designer, and Chief Governing Relationship manager have shared three critical characteristics:

1. A very positive attitude toward their board, viewing it as a precious organizational asset that they are accountable for developing and deploying in the interest of their organization's long-term success

2. In-depth knowledge and expertise in the complex, rapidly evolving field of nonprofit and public governance

3. A view of governing as a top-tier CEO priority

ASSET DEVELOPER AND PARTNER

I've become adept at telling pretty quickly whether a CEO is board savvy enough to succeed at building a really close, positive, and productive working relationship with her board. As a consultant, I've got a large stake in making an accurate assessment since the success of governance consulting engagements depends heavily on the board savviness of the leader at the organizational helm. In this regard, attitude is one of my top-tier criteria. That's why I always ask a CEO I'm considering working with at our first meeting to tell me about his working relationship with the board. If I hear something along these lines, I can feel confident about our becoming partners on the governance front: "They're a great group of people — lots of talent, knowledge, experience, expertise — but, you know, I don't think they're coming close to realizing their potential as a governing body, and I really feel accountable for helping them get to the next level. I know they want to do a better job of governing, but they're just not sure how to go about doing it. I think we've got a pretty good working relationship, but I know it could be better, and I've got a gut sense that if we don't figure out how to get them more engaged in the governing process, it'll jeopardize our relationship."

By contrast, a few years ago I made a snap decision not to work with a CEO whose response to my question was something like this: "As boards go, they're not all that bad. At least they know enough to stay out of my business, so I can't really complain about micromanagement. For example, they adopted next year's budget in a special board meeting a couple of weeks ago, and I'm pleased to report that it only took thirty-five minutes or so. Of course, we — the staff and I — had done a great job of putting the document together, so they couldn't easily quibble about it. That's what I really like in a board: let us do the detailed staff work, keep at a high level, and generally leave us alone to do our jobs. I'll make sure they get the information they need, when they need it, to make decisions, and it's their job to get the decisions made, not mine."

In my experience, truly board-savvy CEOs view their board as a precious organizational asset — perhaps their organization's preeminent resource — and they feel strongly accountable for helping their board become a more effective governing body, and hence a more valuable asset. They really do believe in strong board leadership and want their board to get better at doing its governing work. I've never known a board-savvy CEO to bemoan the motley crew of board members she's been saddled with and express the heartfelt wish to contain the damage they might do if not closely watched. Well aware that the kind of people who get to the boardroom tend to bring good intentions with them, but also to jump in and fill vacuums wherever they find them, the board-savvy CEO asks, "How can I help them become fully engaged in doing really important governing work so that there's no vacuum to fill?" I've also learned that board-savvy CEOs don't think about their board in we-they terms. They know that they've got to be heavily involved in the governing process, functioning as a real governing partner with their board. In fact, an extraordinarily board-savvy CEO I was chatting with recently told me that he considered the chief executive a hybrid position: part board, part staff, and that he thought of himself as, in effect, a board member, albeit without a vote.

Nor does the board-savvy CEO sit around obsessing about the specter of micromanagement. On the contrary, board-savvy CEOs know that governing involves so much intensive board-staff interaction and collaboration that it doesn't make sense to waste time worrying about potential breaches of hard-and-fast boundaries; indeed, they don't see the boundaries as all that hard or fast. I'm reminded of an outstanding board-savvy CEO I worked with a few years ago who exemplified such nondefensive leadership in working with her board. I was sitting in on a special daylong work session involving the board, this CEO, and the executive team of this large children's services nonprofit, which operated out of several locations around the region. The purpose was to review and assess progress in implementing a high-stakes change initiative the board had adopted a month ago: phasing out a residential program and facility that had been at the heart of the agency's mission for seventy-five years. Shortly after our lunch break, we got involved in a very detailed discussion about one of the major implementation challenges: static from several old-time staff members and other key stakeholders, including some prominent donors and two local newspapers. About thirty minutes into this very important and most interesting discussion, one of the board members, feeling guilty, said something like this: "I think we're getting into dangerous territory now. I know you all agree with me that the board should be primarily focused on what we do, not how we do it, and it seems to me that we're getting pretty deeply into the how. Maybe we should leave this to our CEO and her staff."

Despite wearing my consultant hat, I kept quiet, curious how the CEO — a very strong, self-confident executive with a commanding presence — would react. I couldn't have been more pleased when I heard her say she was quite comfortable with board members being involved in the discussion, since the stakes were tremendously high and she and her team needed board members' best thinking. Then, on the spot, she recommended that they spend the next couple of hours analyzing the issues that three key stakeholders — staff, donors, and the media — appeared to have with the phasing out of the residential program, how they might go about handling the issues, and where board members might be able to pitch in and help deal with specific issues. Here, indeed, was a truly board-savvy CEO at work! Were board members actually getting involved in what might traditionally be considered administrative details? To an extent, perhaps. Did it bother the CEO? Not a whit. Board members had valuable wisdom to share about a high-stakes matter and could very likely lend some hands-on assistance in resolving stakeholder issues. So why worry about a hypothetical barrier being breached?

Experience has made me an optimist where human growth is concerned; I've seen many CEOs develop a more positive and productive attitude toward the governance function and their boards, and accordingly reap the benefits in terms of both higher-impact governing and a more solid working relationship with their boards. However, it's important to keep in mind that attitude, being skin-deep emotionally speaking, can all too easily be sabotaged by deeper emotions if the CEO isn't aware of them. The most board-savvy CEOs I've worked with over the years consciously cultivate the kind of emotional self-awareness that protects against self-sabotage in their work with board members. Here's a real-life example. I worked with the CEO of an international trade association for over a year. When I got to know him as a friend, I recognized that he grappled with a deep-seated, powerful need for control in his interactions with people, including board members. Where the board was concerned, what came naturally to him was meticulous preparation for making decisions — every *t* crossed and *i* dotted. He felt such a tremendous need to have the right decision made that he could easily have failed to involve board members in the kind of participatory process that breeds feelings of ownership. However, being keenly aware of his need for control, he was able to discipline himself into designing and facilitating intensive board involvement in the decision-making process, which paid off not only in terms of substantive input but also in the degree of board ownership that was generated.

One of the most egregious examples of self-sabotage that comes to my mind is the CEO of a very prestigious aging services nonprofit I worked with that operated a nursing home and research institute. She had no problem intellectually recognizing that her board was inadequately engaged in the governing process and, therefore, that her board members felt little ownership of, and commitment to, critical governing decisions, so she enthusiastically enlisted my help in designing and facilitating a daylong retreat aimed at strengthening board involvement. She also recognized that the recommendations emerging from the retreat, including the creation of a modern committee structure, made sense in terms of stronger board engagement. However, when it came to actually implementing the recommendations, she couldn't muster up the energy to shepherd them through the final decision-making process. In retrospect, I plead guilty to underestimating her tremendous need for control, which made stronger board involvement a threatening prospect. Without, I'm sure, being fully conscious of what she was doing, she let the recommendations sink beneath the waves from lack of strong CEO support.

WORLD-CLASS EXPERT

Every board-savvy CEO I've worked with has understood the governing business inside out — the detailed nature of governing work, the architecture of the board in terms of its governing role and structure, and the processes for board engagement in key governing areas, such as planning and performance monitoring. As governing aficionados, they stay abreast of advances in the rapidly developing field of nonprofit/public governance — for example, the move away from traditional comprehensive long-range planning as a process for board involvement in strategic decision making, and the emergence of a leaner, more issue-focused approach to planning explicitly aimed at accomplishing strategic change. They're avid consumers of books and articles dealing with governance, and they seek out workshops offering nuts-and-bolts guidance on governance matters.

The compelling reason for a CEO's becoming a world-class expert in governance is obvious: to be able to play the roles of Chief Board Capacity Builder and Chief Governing Process Designer effectively. For example, if a CEO isn't familiar with current thinking about board standing committees as a vehicle for getting the detailed work of governing accomplished, how can that CEO help the board update or fine-tune its governing structure? Equally important, without a firm grasp of the rapidly evolving field of nonprofit and public governance, how could a CEO help her board avoid taking steps that might actually work against high-impact governing? This is extremely important because the field of nonprofit/public governance involves much more art than science. The literature has been relatively scant until recently, and there still isn't a universally accepted body of governance principles and standards that boards and CEOs can follow. On the contrary, governing principles and methodologies are frequently hotly debated, and the number of what I call "fallacious little golden rules" that are floating around in the governance universe can easily lead unwary consumers, including CEOs, astray — all too often even jeopardizing their positions.

To take a real-life example: one fallacious little golden rule that

I've seen do considerable damage to the cause of high-impact governing is that small boards are more effective governing bodies than larger ones. A couple of years ago, I came across a national association that had recently downsized its board from approximately twenty-five members to seven. The rationale behind this wrongheaded — although strongly recommended by a consultant — move was governing efficiency. The logic went something like this: the twenty-five-member board was proving to be an inefficient governing body, getting few really important governing decisions made; the apparent reason was that a board that large was too unwieldy and inefficient; ergo, the board needed to be dramatically downsized. What seemed like a no-brainer solution wouldn't have gotten by a really board-savvy CEO, who would have recognized, in the first place, that a twenty-five-member board allowed for healthy diversity in terms of knowledge, expertise, experience, perspectives, and stakeholder representation. This board-savvy CEO would also have recognized that such diversity could be put to work in many important ways, such as making high-stakes strategic decisions and burnishing the nonprofit's image.

A truly board-savvy CEO would also have known that the twenty-five-member board could have relatively easily been transformed into a very effective — and diverse! — governing body by clarifying its governing role, employing a well-designed committee structure, and mapping out processes for meaningful board involvement in decision making. The bottom line in this unfortunate case: accomplishing a minor-league goal — governing efficiency — at the expense of a tremendously important goal — board diversity. I should also point out another cost of achieving this minor-league efficiency, for the CEO at least: a board far easier for a passionate cadre of single-issue board members to hijack, as superintendents with boards of only five or seven members have painfully learned.

TOP-TIER CEO PRIORITY

Every board-savvy CEO I've worked with over the years has treated governing as one of her top chief executive functions, typically along with strategic decision making, financial resource development, and external/stakeholder relations. In practical terms, this obviously means making a significant time commitment to working with the board — in my experience between 25 and 30 percent of a CEO's time on the average. Where the time commitment is concerned, I strongly counsel rigorous self-auditing to make sure the time is actually being spent on governing matters since self-deception is always a clear and present danger. I've come across more than one CEO who's convinced himself that he's devoting significant time to governing when, in reality, he's put it lower on the list than CEO functions that feel more familiar, comfortable and satisfying, such as strategic planning or cultivating donors.

I worked closely on a couple of occasions with a woman who was in many ways a brilliant CEO — visionary, extremely bright, highly innovative, and extraordinarily energetic. There's no question she believed in the importance of high-quality governing, as evidenced by her taking the lead in helping her board update its governing role and modernize its standing committee structure. But it turned out to be extremely difficult for her to devote sustained attention to the governing function, and as a result the new committee structure ended up being only tenuously established and consequently seriously underperforming. What really struck me was that she appeared genuinely unaware that governing was taking a back seat to priorities that titillated her executive palate.

It's also important to keep in mind that a CEO's devoting at least 25 percent of her time to the governing function won't mean it's a top CEO priority in practice unless that time is thoughtfully allocated. Otherwise, it's all too easy for a CEO to spend a disproportionate amount of his governing time doing what comes naturally or feels familiar and comfortable. A few years ago, I worked with a CEO who was a consummate people-person who loved — and was very good at — schmoozing with board members. There's no question his interpersonal skills played an important part in building a positive working relationship with the board, and I've seen many a CEO whose cold and aloof style alienated many board members. But, predictably, overreliance on schmoozing and inattention to such critical matters as figuring out how to engage the board meaningfully in strategic decision making eventually resulted in a parting of the ways between this affable CEO and his board. By the way, I've seen just as many cases of CEOs whose inattention to the interpersonal dimension has eroded their working relationship with the board despite their mastery of the "harder" aspects of governing.

I've learned a very useful technique from board-savvy CEOs who have employed it with great success behind the scenes: acting as the "executive director" of the governing "program," which encompasses the board, all of its governing processes, and the staff work involved in preparing for — and following up on — committee and full board meetings. Thinking of the governing function as a very important program that the CEO is responsible for managing is a practical way of translating the priority into actual practice. One CEO I know who makes effective use of this technique devotes a couple of hours every weekend to assessing program progress and doing program planning in two areas:

Ongoing board operations: How is the governing process functioning? What issues have come up that need attention (for example, lagging attendance at planning committee meetings or inadequate staff preparation for finance committee meetings)? How should they be addressed (for example, bringing the attendance issue up at the next governance committee meeting for discussion)? What major governing events are on the horizon that need special attention (for example, the annual strategic planning work session, which needs to be on the agenda of the next executive team meeting to ensure adequate preparation)?

Long-term board development: What serious long-term board development issues are emerging, such as the need for an updated board role description, or an inadequate process for recruiting new board members, which is resulting in an increasingly "birds-of-a-feather" board dangerously lacking in diversity? What steps need to be taken to deal with the emerging issues, such as impaneling a governance task force or holding a special governance work session? What's the most effective way to bring these developmental issues to the board's attention, for example, jointly with the board chair at the next governance committee meeting?

ANYONE CAN BECOME MORE BOARD SAVVY

One of the key premises of this book is that board savviness can be learned. If I didn't really believe that, writing this book would have been an exercise in futility. I haven't yet run into a CEO who couldn't become more board savvy if he or she really wanted to; it's a pretty straightforward process of acquiring the requisite knowledge and skills and mustering the will and maybe even the courage to put the knowledge and skills to work. Unfortunately, many executives are unlikely to acquire the knowledge and skills on the job, as they ascend the professional ladder on their way to the CEO suite — unless they are fortunate enough to be the mentees of board-savvy CEOs who feel morally obliged to help them develop their board savviness. For one thing, many CEO-aspirants don't have enough sustained interaction with their board to learn a lot about governing firsthand. For another, many of the qualities that help CEO-aspirants climb the organizational ladder (for example, doing finished staff work, with all the loose ends tied up) end up being counterproductive when working with a board. And waiting to learn on the job once reaching the top spot is extraordinarily difficult and more than a little risky. This, in a nutshell, is why I've written *The Board-Savvy CEO*.

But I'm obliged to share some bad news. Just because you're an avid student who's mastered the content in this book, you shouldn't expect that applying what you've learned will be a piece of cake. Consistently behaving in a board-savvy manner is very likely to require a large dollop of discipline and tenacity and perhaps on occasion a fair amount of courage. For one thing, it might feel counterintuitive and maybe even dangerous. Many CEOs and CEO-aspirants — especially the ones who see a hard-and-fast line separating the board's governing role from the CEO's executive management role and who can easily conjure up the specter of board micromanagement — might very well find working more collaboratively with their boards to get high-impact governing done a nerve-racking, threatening experience. And, of course, every CEO and CEO-aspirant reading this book is already tremendously busy, so finding the time to build a closer, more collaborative and productive partnership with the board will inevitably require reducing other CEO commitments. It took tremendous effort and tenacity, and no little courage, on Jeff Finkle's part, for example, to work closely with representatives of the boards of the American Economic Development Council and the Council for Urban Economic Development to consummate the merger that resulted in the International Economic Development Council. Jeff will tell you that the effort was worth it, no question: IEDC is now the world's preeminent economic development association. But Jeff would be the first to testify that getting it done stretched him to the limit.

CHAPTER TWO

———————

THE BOARD-SAVVY CEO AS CHIEF BOARD CAPACITY BUILDER

THE LAY OF THE GOVERNING LAND

This chapter examines how the board-savvy CEO can — and definitely should — play the leading role as what I call the Chief Board Capacity Builder in developing the board's capacity to do the kind of high-impact governing work that makes a significant difference in organizational affairs. More specifically, in this chapter I explore how the board-savvy CEO can spearhead the process of the board's updating what we can think of as its governing design: its governing role; its governing structure; and its self-management capacity. After describing some of the major barriers board-savvy CEOs are likely to encounter in playing the Chief Board Capacity Builder role, this chapter:

- explains how the board-savvy CEO can go about enlisting board Change Champions to spearhead the process of updating the board's governing design;

- describes two powerful approaches to involving board members in the design process: the governance retreat and the governance task force; and

- takes a close look at the substantive content of the four key elements of the board's governing design: the board's governing role; the board's governing structure; the board's composition; and the board's performance-management capacity.

Before we travel farther along the board development road, this is an appropriate place to take a look at the nature of nonprofit and public boards generally and the content of their governing work. As we begin this brief tour of the governing terrain, it's important to keep in mind that all boards — whether they are public or nonprofit, large or small, engaged in association management, health care, public transportation, economic development or another of the many areas public and nonprofit boards are engaged in — are fundamentally alike in one respect. Every board is, by definition, an organization within the wider organization it's part of (for example, the Board of Directors of the International Economic Development Council or of Evergreen Life Services): a formally established, permanent entity consisting of people who are engaged, within a framework of formal policies and procedures, in accomplishing a particular mission — to govern. "Who cares?" you might be tempted to ask. Well, it's important to keep in mind because, as an organizational unit, the board — like any other organizational unit within the wider organization, such as the office of the CEO, the educational services department, or the finance department — can be consciously developed or designed to make it more effective and efficient in carrying out its governing mission. In fact, not paying close, systematic attention to developing the board as a governing organization would be a surefire path to diminished board governing performance over the long run. Now let's take a look at the work that the governing organization known as the board does.

GOVERNING IN A NUTSHELL

One of the questions I always ask when I interview board members one-on-one early in a consulting engagement is "What's your definition of governing?" More often than not, I initially get a pretty nebulous answer, like "policy making" or "setting directions for our organization." When I probe a bit, I tend to hear things like "We set overall goals," or "We make sure staff are doing their jobs," or "We hire and fire the CEO." What I seldom hear is a well-thought-out, comprehensive description of the work of governing, which has led me to conclude that many, if not most, board members don't really have a very good handle on their governing work. I'm not sure it really matters whether the average board member can come up with a comprehensive, detailed definition of governing work on the spot, but I do know for sure that a truly board-savvy CEO must have an in-depth understanding of the board's governing work if she is to be an effective partner with her board. Let me first define the work of governing a nonprofit generally and then drill down a bit to take a more nuts-and-bolts look at this preeminent board responsibility. Interestingly, you'll see that policy making per se is a relatively tiny part of governing.

GOVERNING AT A HIGH LEVEL

What a board does at the highest level when it governs is to answer — on an ongoing basis — four very fundamental questions:

1. What do we want our nonprofit to become over the long haul, in terms of our programs and services, our customers and clients, our revenue mix, our geographical reach, our position relative to competitors, and so on? You can call this the strategic planning

question, which involves visioning and long-range strategic planning of some kind.

2. What do we want our nonprofit to be now and over the coming year, in terms of what we do, whom we serve, and what we spend? This is the operational planning question that has to do with the nonprofit's mission and the current and next year's annual operating plan/budget.

3. How are we doing, in terms of delivering services and products to our customers and clients, managing our operations, making use of technology, and maintaining relationships with key stakeholders and the public at large? This is the accountability question, having to do with making judgments based on reviewing programmatic and financial performance reports.

4. What rules should guide and constrain our organization in governing and carrying out our operational responsibilities? This is the policy-making question, and the board answers the question by putting new policies in place and periodically updating existing policies. For example, the nonprofit's bylaws would be at the pinnacle of policy making, followed by broad rules governing major areas of operation, such as financial management, human resources, and contracting. Unless a nonprofit is involved in a major overhaul of its policy structure, I estimate that keeping policies updated and filling policy gaps makes up around 5 percent of a board's ongoing governing work.

GOVERNING AT A MORE NUTS-AND-BOLTS LEVEL

From board meeting to board meeting, there's nothing theoretically exotic about the work of governing a nonprofit, although the work is often very complex and demanding. What the board essentially does is to make decisions about concrete governing "products" (for example, adopting an updated values and vision statement or an annual operating plan and budget), and it also makes judgments based on such governing information as a quarterly financial report comparing actual to budgeted expenditures for a particular period or a program performance report documenting what's been accomplished compared to the goals the nonprofit has set. You'll come across the term "high-impact governing" often in these pages. High-impact boards do a very effective job of making the highest-stakes decisions and judgments that have a significant impact on organizational affairs. I briefly described some truly high-impact governing decisions earlier in this chapter, such as the decision of two boards to merge, creating the International Economic Development Council, and the Evergreen Life Services Board's adopting the strategic initiative to invest in social enterprises that would add earned income to Evergreen's revenue mix.

Keep in mind that these ongoing decisions and judgments that make up the detailed governing work of every nonprofit board are often quite complex and difficult to make. It takes a board-savvy CEO to play the leading role in helping the board map out the processes for getting governing decisions made on the basis of good information and in such a fashion that they contribute to board members' satisfaction and feelings of ownership.

GOVERNING: AN UNRULY TEAM SPORT

"Boards make policy decisions; the CEO and staff carry them out. Boards decide the *what*, and the CEO and staff take care of the *how*. Boards should focus on ends, and the CEO and staff on means." These pithy descriptions of the division of labor between the governing body and its CEO and staff probably sound pretty familiar. They certainly appear countless times in my notes of interviews with board members and CEOs. Elegant in their simplicity, these role delineations are not, broadly speaking, wrong, but being slogan-like statements that are abstracted from reality, they are definitely of no practical use in the day-to-day work of governing a nonprofit or public organization. In fact, because they suggest that you could even draw a solid line separating the governing work of boards from the executive and administrative work of CEOs and their staff, these abstract guidelines can be misleading and even dangerous, leading to a simplistic we-they view of the governing terrain that can all-too-easily preempt serious thinking about how we can get the complex work of governing done.

Board-savvy CEOs are above all else clear-headed realists who know, first, that governing a nonprofit or public organization is a team sport whose players are board members, the CEO, and her top lieutenants and, second, that governing is a messy game without hard-and-fast boundaries separating the different players' roles. I've defined governing as making decisions about concrete governing products such as a values and vision statement or the annual operating plan and budget and making judgments based on such governing information as a quarterly financial report. Truly board-savvy CEOs know that the processes for making these decisions and judgments involve intensive collaboration and interaction among the key governing team players — board, CEO, and executive staff. Experience has taught them that very little of the work involved in getting a complex governing decision made — such as adopting the annual budget — is "pure" board or staff work; rather the bulk of the work involves the active collaboration of board and staff members sitting at the same table.

I'm reminded of an experience early in my consulting career that taught me a valuable lesson about the intensive board-staff collaboration involved in making complex governing decisions — and about transcending the negative we-they mindset. My client, a large suburban school district, was gearing up for the annual budget preparation process. The board's newly formed planning committee, along with the superintendent and a few of his top lieutenants, met to go over the budget preparation calendar, pinpointing when the committee and full board would be involved in the process. Before getting into the details, planning committee members made clear that they were fed up with the board's lack of meaningful involvement in the budget process in recent years. The committee chair pointed out that the board's traditional role basically consisted of thumbing through the finished budget document that the superintendent transmitted a month before the budget adoption deadline. At that point in the game, as everyone in the meeting recognized, all board members could do was ask relatively unimportant questions about particular line items. Raising critical issues at that point would wreak havoc, and no one wanted that.

The superintendent, a truly board-savvy CEO, wasn't taken aback by the criticism. Far from being thrown on the defensive, he welcomed the opportunity to brainstorm a new process with more timely and meaningful board involvement. The upshot was a daylong prebudget work session involving the school board, superintendent, and all of his executive team, which took place before department heads began putting their detailed budgets together. There were two primary objectives. The first was to analyze the key factors driving expenditure levels — both controllable (such as salary increases) and uncontrollable (such as utility costs) — and to determine what major cost decisions needed to be made and how and when in the process they would be made. The second was to identify and discuss operational planning issues at the department level, based on presentations by all of the department heads, and to reach agreement on the issues that would receive special attention in the proposed budget document. The issue analysis part of the work session, as it turned out, was eye-opening to board members, who realized that many important operational issues (for example, growing violence at high school football games) could be addressed through the budget process without necessarily increasing expenditures.

THE NONGOVERNING WORK OF BOARDS

Nonprofit board members are often engaged in doing important nongoverning work, typically when it's been determined that board members are uniquely qualified to contribute and/or there aren't sufficient staff to get this nongoverning work done alone. Several boards I've worked with in recent years, for example, regularly schedule board members to speak in important forums, such as a chamber of commerce luncheon or a state legislative committee considering regulations affecting the nonprofit, as a very important way to educate the wider public and important stakeholders about the nonprofit's goals and accomplishments and, in the legislative case, to influence policy making. Another nongoverning activity that many boards have gotten involved in is hands-on fund-raising (as contrasted with the true governing work of setting revenue targets, adopting fund-raising strategies, and monitoring fund-raising performance).

The board-savvy CEOs I've worked with and observed over the

years don't have a problem with their board members getting involved in important nongoverning work so long as board members are actually needed to do the specific nongoverning work; board members are well qualified to do it; and the nongoverning work will not seriously compete with and detract from the board's fundamental mission: making governing decisions and judgments. Board-savvy CEOs are always aware of the danger of overextending and possibly burning out board members by loading too much nongoverning work on top of the demanding job of governing. This is an important reason why, in my experience, it can be extremely difficult to fill positions on so-called "doing boards." Board-savvy CEOs also well know that overloading their board with nongoverning work actually works against nonboard volunteer engagement. The International Economic Development Council, for example, has tremendously expanded nonboard volunteer involvement by uncoupling board members from several traditional "doing" committees engaged in such nongoverning activities as planning the annual meeting and developing educational programs, thereby freeing up space for nonboard member volunteers to become engaged.

A STARK CHOICE: INHERIT OR CONSCIOUSLY DESIGN

The board and CEO of every nonprofit and public organization face a stark choice: Either inherit the board of the past, in terms of its organizational structure and practices, moving yesterday's board into the future largely unchanged, or consciously and systematically develop the board's capacity as a governing organization by updating its governing design — its role, structure, and self-management. I would love to report that the great majority of boards and CEOs choose the systematic capacity-building path, but all I can say with assurance is that many don't, and the following true story is all-too-common in my experience.

"Well, that's the way it's been for as long as I've been on the board, and I can't recall that we've ever talked about it. It's working alright I guess; at least I'm not aware of any big problems. But, to be honest, I haven't really given the matter much thought." I'm paraphrasing the comments of a board member of a prestigious aging services non-profit that operates a skilled nursing home and assisted living facility, in response to a question I asked during the interview phase of a board development initiative: "What's the rationale for the approach you and your board colleagues take to filling vacancies on the board?" In fact, despite this board member's not perceiving any problems with the process, it was a woefully inadequate approach to renewing the board's composition. Nominating committee members over the course of two or three meetings sat around talking about people they knew who might be willing to serve on the board, without using any kind of profile of desired attributes and qualifications to come up with likely candidates. The inevitable result of this who-knows-whom approach was a stunningly undiverse birds-of-a-feather board. And adding insult to injury, the absence of board member term limits ensured not only lack of diversity but also a collective hardening of the governing arteries.

STANDING IN THE WAY

Why do so many nonprofit and public boards merely inherit the board of the past and move it into the future largely unimproved? Five interrelated barriers to systematic board capacity building appear to loom largest: inertia; ego investment; fear; lack of commitment; and an un-board-savvy CEO. As was certainly the case of the birds-of-a-feather board example cited above, inertia, which might well be the most powerful factor working against systematic board development, is typically the result of both comfort and ignorance. For one thing, board members feel comfortable with the board's current functioning and don't see any particularly important problems. And the primary reason they don't see problems is they lack awareness of both the need for change and concrete change possibilities.

Members of the birds-of-a-feather board, for example, are not only comfortable with the undiverse board they've created and maintained, they are ignorant of the need for an infusion of new blood and unaware of practical steps they might take to achieve greater diversity. Two pertinent sayings come to mind: "Ignorance is bliss" and the pernicious "If it ain't broke, don't fix it." In a nutshell: "We like it the way it is, thank you, we don't see any compelling reason to change."

Ego investment in the way things are is one of the preeminent barriers to board capacity building. To take a real-life example: a retired former high-ranking bank executive — let's call him "Hank" — had been chair of the regional transit authority's finance committee for all seven years he'd served on the authority's board. In the eyes of his board colleagues, he was "Mr. Finance," and he loved the role, especially when he was immersed in the process of annual budget preparation. When the board's governance task force recommended that Hank's finance committee be folded into the new performance oversight and monitoring committee, he instantly became a visceral opponent of the new committee, making clear to his colleagues that it was an incredibly stupid idea.

Since the rationale behind the recommendation was clearly sound (combining like functions — monitoring financial and operational performance and identifying financial and operational issues needing attention), and Hank was nothing if not bright, the obvious explanation for Hank's passionate and wrongheaded opposition was a threatened ego. Retired from a high-ranking position he'd loved, he couldn't stand the prospect of losing one of his few remaining sources of ego satisfaction. His support, by the way, was ultimately "bought" by offering him the chairmanship of the new committee.

Fear is another major barrier to board development that I've encountered numerous times in my work with nonprofits, more often than not, fear of being found wanting in a new role and possibly suffering the embarrassment of public failure. I encountered this recently when working with the newly created planning committee of an association board. One of the committee's preeminent responsibilities was oversight of the annual budget preparation process, which had traditionally been the bailiwick of the chief financial officer, who'd every year just send a finished budget document to the old-time finance committee, which after thumbing through and tweaking it a bit, sent it along to the board for adoption. The new planning committee was explicitly charged with figuring out ways to engage the whole board early in the budget preparation process so that they could help shape, rather than just react to, the budget. The strong reluctance of three of the committee members to getting involved in budget preparation made sense only from the perspective of fear. In fact, one of the three actually told me in a sidebar conversation at the new committee's inaugural meeting, "We'll look like idiots trying to guide budgeting; we just plain don't know enough!" You'd better believe it took a lot of hand-holding by the committee chair and the chief financial officer to stiffen the backbones of these three reluctant committee members.

Fortunately, what are known as "letterhead" board members — those who are in the governing game primarily to embellish their professional resume or pump up their ego and whose commitment to governing is consequently skin-deep — are, in my experience, few and far between. But they do pop up now and then, and they can be counted on to resist any attempt to develop the board's governing capacity for the simple reason that the board development effort will appear likely to call for a larger commitment of time and effort down the road than they are prepared to make. As one of these letterhead board members observed in a meeting to discuss the need for systematic board development, "No one ever mentioned that we'd be spending time overhauling the board when I was recruited, and I certainly didn't bargain for this!" And the fifth significant roadblock in the way of systematic board capacity building is a CEO who isn't board savvy enough to take the lead in board capacity building.

TURNING-POINT GOVERNING DESIGN VERSUS FINE-TUNING

A year or so after she became the President and CEO of the Miami Lighthouse for the Blind and Visually Impaired, Virginia Jacko realized that major change would be required to turn the Lighthouse Board into a high-impact governing body capable of meeting the challenges facing the Lighthouse and serving as a strong partner with her on the Lighthouse's Strategic Governing Team. Uncertainty about the board's governing role, a recent history of meddling in Lighthouse administrative matters, the absence of a contemporary committee structure aligned with the board's major governing responsibilities, and the almost complete absence of board self-management (for example, monitoring and evaluating the board's performance) — these were issues that defied a quick fix and that an incremental fine-tuning approach couldn't possibly have addressed. Therefore, Virginia and the board officers launched a governance task force that over the course of three months or so came up with a comprehensive set of recommendations to transform the board into a governing powerhouse.

This kind of turning-point board capacity building is the focus of this chapter. It deals with such fundamental questions as: What are our board's principal governing responsibilities and functions? How big should our board be? How should we go about filling vacancies on our board to ensure the kind of composition we need to govern effectively? What board standing committees do we need to accomplish the detailed work of governing? Once a public or nonprofit organization like the Miami Lighthouse has gone through a well-designed turning-point capacity-building process and has implemented the governance enhancements generated by the process, then a more incremental, fine-tuning approach should suffice from year to year — until major environmental change forces the organization to go through another in-depth capacity-building effort. In Chapter Three, I'll explore in detail how well-designed board standing committees can handle ongoing board fine-tuning, serving as continuous governing improvement engines.

DONNING THE CHIEF BOARD CAPACITY BUILDER HAT

Board members must be intensively involved in updating their board's governing design — the board's composition; its governing role; and its governing structure — if they are to feel the degree of ownership that will fuel implementation of the design, but they can't realistically be expected to play the leading role in the updating process. As part-time volunteers who are typically engaged in active careers separate from their board service, they bring neither the time nor the governing knowledge and expertise required to take the lead in board capacity building. Only a truly board-savvy CEO can muster the resources required to play the Chief Board Capacity Builder role effectively: substantial time; in-depth technical governing knowledge; and access to executive staff technical support. And, of course, by virtue of her position, the CEO brings the stature necessary to work as a colleague with board members in board capacity building. Wearing the Chief Board Capacity Builder hat, the board-savvy CEO plays a leading role in:

- building a cadre of change champions on the board who play a major, visible role in the governing design process, including building an appetite among other board members for tackling capacity building and legitimizing the capacity-building process;

- working with the board change champions to put in place — and secure the full board's commitment to — a process for accomplishing the turning-point governing design work, while also fostering the kind of board member ownership that fuels commitment to change;

- providing technical support for the capacity-building process, making sure that it generates concrete recommendations for updating the board's governing design; and

- managing implementation of the recommended governing enhancements, working closely with her senior executives.

TRANSFORMING THE BOARD CHAIR INTO A CHANGE CHAMPION

In Chapter One, I describe board members who are satisfied owners of their governing work as one of the surefire signs of a board-savvy CEO at work in a nonprofit or public organization. You can think of board change champions as hyperowners, who aren't only committed to updating their board's governing design but are signed on as strong advocates and cheerleaders for the design process, playing the leading role in convincing their board colleagues to join in the governing design process. Enlisting these hyperowners is one of the preeminent responsibilities of the board-savvy CEO, wearing the Chief Board Capacity Builder hat. Jeff Finkle, long-time president and CEO of the International Economic Development Council, and Lana Vukovljak, former president and CEO of the American Association of Diabetes Educators, were extraordinarily successful at enlisting board change champions in updating their associations' governing designs. Both Jeff and Lana first recruited their board chair to serve as a primo change champion and then, working closely with their chair, brought other officers on board as champions.

Failing to take this first critical step — transforming the board chair into a change champion — can be fatal to board capacity building, if not immediately, then down the road a bit. I saw this happen a few years ago, when the CEO of a public transportation authority pushed forward with a governance improvement initiative — kicked off by a daylong retreat of all board members, the CEO, and executive team — without having gotten his board chair's firm commitment to serve as change champion #1. In fact, the board chair's lack of enthusiasm was palpable. He not only didn't ever make an unambiguous commitment to see the governing design update process through, he even more than once let the CEO know early on that he thought there were pressing priorities that outweighed board capacity building. As it turned out, the CEO, feeling that the board development initiative couldn't be delayed, pressed ahead, assuming his board chair would become a strong champion as the process moved forward. Unfortunately, after a highly successful retreat and the development of a set of concrete recommendations for updating the board's role and structure, the process came to a halt in the face of the chair's reluctance to spend more time on capacity building. An opportunity was missed, and, sad to say, the CEO's credibility was seriously damaged.

Turning the board chair into an ardent change champion is one of the fine arts of board-savvy CEOship. Jeff, Lana, and other board-savvy CEOs I've worked with over the years have accomplished this first critical step in the board capacity-building process by pursuing two critical strategies.

They educate the board chair, making sure that she understands the key characteristics of high-impact governing boards — for example, by going to governing workshops together and sharing pertinent books and articles — and that their chair also becomes aware of the gap between the ideal high-impact governing board and their particular board and the concrete capacity-building steps other boards have taken to close similar gaps.

They also appeal to the board chair's altruism and ego, making sure, first, that the chair understands the stakes involved in board capacity building, namely that higher-impact governing decisions will be critical to future organizational stability and growth; second, that the board chair realizes that the capacity-building initiative is one of those rare opportunities to leave an imprint — a legacy — in the form of a higher-functioning governing board; and, third, that she recognizes that her visible leadership is essential to significant, successful change on the governance front. For example, I found in my client files this morning the copy of an e-mail the truly board-savvy CEO of an aging services nonprofit sent to his board chair after they'd returned from a state association conference, which said in part:

> I know you and I agree that we've got to beef up the Board's governing role and come up with a structure to help them get their governing work done, and I'm really looking forward to working closely with you to get our

Board development initiative on the road. As we discussed on the drive back last night, there's no way we'll get the Board's buy-in without you being our preeminent cheerleader for the effort, and I'm really grateful you're going to step up to the plate. What a wonderful opportunity for you, as our Board Chair, to leave the legacy of a top-tier governing body when your term ends!

I'm pleased to report that, in my experience, the great majority of board chairs really do want to make a strong contribution to the organizations they have signed on to govern, and when you consider that the chair's role tends to be long on ceremony and short on substantive content, the idea of championing a worthy cause and leaving a substantial leadership legacy behind can be immensely appealing. That said, actually transforming the chair into a solid champion for governing change can require a large dollop of CEO strategy and time. By the way, I'm often asked in governance workshops I'm presenting for CEOs what to do if the board chair is truly a lost cause. My response: Make a serious effort to enlist your chair as the #1 champion for governing change, giving it your best shot. But if it becomes clear that despite your best thinking and effort your chair doesn't have the makings of an effective champion, then bide your time and hope your next chair is a more suitable candidate for champion in chief. What you can't afford to do is what the transportation CEO I described above did: plow ahead and hope the chair miraculously rises to the occasion. Of course, miracles do happen, but they appear to be pretty rare in human affairs.

With the board chair having agreed to play the role of change champion in chief, what board-savvy CEOs like Jeff Finkle and Lana Vukovljak have done is work with their chair in turning other board officers, who normally make up the board's executive or governance committee, into champions for updating the board's governing design. In addition to education (for example, describing what a high-impact governing board looks like and pinpointing the gaps separating their board from the model high-impact board) and altruism (inviting them to join in making a powerful contribution in terms of effective leadership), experience has taught that offering board officers a lead role in the design process can be a strong incentive, as I discuss below.

TWO POWERFUL APPROACHES

Board-savvy CEOs well know, as I pointed out in Chapter One, that board members who are satisfied owners of their governing work make for more reliable members of the Strategic Governing Team and that ownership is a feeling that primarily comes from meaningful involvement in shaping governing decisions and judgments. Two of the most powerful processes for getting a nonprofit or public organization's governing design updated while also generating the kind of board ownership that fuels commitment to implementing the design recommendations generated by the process are the retreat-driven design approach and the task force-driven approach. The retreat-driven approach, which the International and American Associations for Dental Research jointly took, under the leadership of their board-savvy CEO, Christopher Fox, is preferable when your board chair and CEO determine that intensive, early involvement of all board members will be critical to the ultimate success of the governance design effort. The IADR/AADR process was highly successful in accomplishing turning-point change in the two boards' roles, including a better-designed committee structure. Later in this chapter,

I'll share substantive examples of governance improvements, but for now I'll describe the features that made the IADR/AADR update effort so successful.

First, the IADR/AADR board chairs created a retreat design committee consisting of the officers of the two associations, who, with the help of a consultant and strong support from Chris Fox, created a detailed design for the daylong governance retreat: its concrete objectives (for example, to familiarize themselves with the key characteristics of high-functioning nonprofit boards; and to identify issues in the form of opportunities to capitalize on these advances in strengthening the two boards as governing bodies); its structure (for example, that it was to include all board members and the whole IADR/AADR management team; that it would be a daylong session; that it would be professionally facilitated; and that it would use breakout groups); the blow-by-blow agenda; and the follow-through process. This critical front-end retreat design job was largely accomplished over the course of a daylong in-person meeting at the IADR/AADR headquarters, followed by a teleconference at which the consultant retained to assist the process presented the write-up of the design, after which it was sent to all board and executive team members who would be participating in the retreat.

Employing breakout groups led by board members (for example, the values and vision clarification group and the external environmental opportunities and challenges group) helped to ensure active board member involvement and thus to build a line of credit consisting of board member ownership and commitment that could be drawn on in implementing governing change. Board breakout group leaders, whom the retreat design committee chose, could not be allowed to falter or fail in playing this very public role; not only would it set the process back technically, it would also earn the enmity of the board members whose underperformance would cause them embarrassment. Therefore, the consultant developed a set of guidelines for running breakout groups and used it in conducting a thorough orientation for the leaders via a teleconference well before the retreat.

Devoting the morning session to strategic planning work — such as brainstorming values and vision and identifying challenges and opportunities — created a context for the afternoon session focusing on governing issues. The design committee felt, correctly I'm sure, that jumping right into developing the board's governing capacity, in the absence of a broader strategic framework, would likely make many board members choke up. Mapping out the follow-through process in detail reassured skeptical board members that the retreat would ultimately be worth all the time, effort, and money being committed to it — that the deliberations would not be written in sand. For example, the consultant retained to help plan and facilitate the retreat was to prepare a detailed set of action recommendations drawing on the retreat deliberations, and the retreat design committee would remain in existence to review the recommendations and present them to the board.

Requiring that the retreat design committee would review the consultant's follow-through recommendations and subsequently present them to the board (with the consultant in a back-up role) ensured an even higher degree of ownership on the part of the Change Champions on the board, while also making the case for adopting the recommendations stronger because of the peer-to-peer interaction. The board presenters employed PowerPoint slides in their presentation of the recommendations to the board, and they diligently rehearsed to ensure they made their points effectively. And, finally, the use of an experienced governance consultant with extensive facilitation experience and in-depth governing knowledge and experience helped to ensure not only that the retreat was capably facilitated but also that the follow-through recommendations were technically sound in the sense of dealing with serious IADR/AADR governing issues while also capitalizing on recent advances in the field of nonprofit and public governance.

The governance task force-driven approach, which IEDC and the Miami Lighthouse successfully employed under the leadership of Jeff Finkle and Virginia Jacko, is different primarily in terms of the starting point. Consisting of the board's officers and the CEO, the Miami Lighthouse governance task force met four or five times over the course of eight weeks — with the assistance of a consultant — familiarizing themselves with the characteristics of high-impact governing bodies, identifying opportunities to strengthen the Miami Lighthouse board's governing capacity, and fashioning concrete change recommendations. As with the IADR/AADR example, the board members on the task force presented carefully crafted and rehearsed recommendations to the full board in a special work session, with their consultant attending as a back up to respond to questions as appropriate.

IADR/AADR, IEDC, and the Miami Lighthouse, along with many other nonprofits headed by board-savvy CEOs, paid close attention to implementation of the recommendations, by creating a board implementation oversight committee — typically the governance task force or retreat design committee with a new name — which was responsible for:

- working with the consultant and CEO in developing a detailed implementation plan dealing with myriad details, such as conducting orientation and training sessions for the new committees being put in place;

- monitoring implementation; and

- dealing with issues as they arose (for example, difficulty finding a board member willing to chair one of the new committees).

BEWARE OF RELYING ON TWO WEAK TOOLS

I've described two of the more powerful approaches to a turning-point design effort. Now I'd like to take a brief look at two relatively weak governance reform tools that can't safely be relied on to get the design job done: board training and board self-assessment.

In my experience, training is generally a weak tool for transforming board members into owners of their governing work, including updating their governing design, and, consequently, can't be expected to generate the degree of commitment required to get design decisions (such as establishing a new committee structure) firmly made and implemented. The reason is simple. Training turns board members into a passive audience, and such passive involvement never fosters ownership. However, training can make a valuable contribution to the design effort in two ways. First, it can assist in building an appetite for tackling the demanding job of accomplishing a major governing design update. For example, Astor Services for Children and Families, under the leadership of its very board-savvy CEO, Jim McGuirk, successfully used a daylong governance educational workshop to make a compelling case for establishing a governance task force to update Astor's governing design. And training can be a useful tool in the context of a well-thought-out governing design process that actively involves board members, for example as the first component of a daylong governance design retreat.

Another dangerously weak tool is the self-assessment survey. I'll never forget a conversation I had five years or so ago with the board chair and CEO of an international professional association. They'd asked me to spend an hour with them on the phone to help them resolve what they called a "perplexing dilemma." It turns out that they'd been working with a consultant representing a nonprofit resource center who'd spent several weeks compiling and assessing the results of a highly detailed self-assessment survey of the association's governing practices, asking participants to assess such factors as the effectiveness of board meetings and the satisfaction they derived from board service on a scale of one (low) to five. The board chair opened our conversation by saying something along the following lines: "We have a mountain of information, and it looks pretty scientific, but we don't have a clue where to go with it."

As it turns out, they did, indeed, have a mountain of information, but it was a molehill in terms of relevance, because of the inherent subjectivity of such self-assessment tools, which are essentially opinion polls. The most they can tell you is what participants are thinking and feeling about particular topics, but it's hard to imagine a less reliable guide to making concrete improvements in a board's role, structure and self-management capacity. What ultimately happened in this instance is that the chair and CEO convinced the board's executive committee to create a governance task force to spearhead a systematic board development process, creating a fiction that it was drawing on the assessment information, which in actuality was sensibly ignored.

THE SUBSTANTIVE DIMENSION OF GOVERNING DESIGN

This chapter has conducted a tour of the nonprofit and public governing terrain and has examined practical ways that board-savvy CEOs, wearing their Chief Board Capacity Builder hat, have employed to transform board members into champions for, and owners of, updating their boards' governing design: its governing role, committee structure, and self-management capacity. I've also described practical vehicles and processes that board-savvy CEOs and their boards have put to good use in accomplishing turning-point governing design updates — the governance retreat and task force. Now I'd like to turn to the substantive dimension — the content — of governing design, describing concrete examples of three key elements of real-life governing design updates: the board's governing role; the board's governing structure; and the board's composition. These examples are only illustrative and are not intended to fit every nonprofit or public organization perfectly. As they say, correctly in my experience, one size never does fit all, and conscientious tailoring to fit particular needs and circumstances always makes sense.

THE BOARD GOVERNING MISSION

Many nonprofit and public strategic governing teams have found it very helpful to clarify their boards' governing role by fashioning a high-level board governing mission as the natural first step in updating their boards' governing design. The board's governing mission is often brainstormed at a retreat, after which it is refined and ultimately adopted by the full board. A kind of high-level board job description, the governing mission describes the board's governing role in terms of its primary governing functions and intended governing outcomes. For example, the governing mission of Evergreen Life Services states that the Evergreen Board is responsible for serving as "the steward and guardian of Evergreen Life Services' values, vision, and mission" and for playing "a leading, proactive role in Evergreen Life Services' strategic decision making, and in setting strong, clear strategic directions and priorities for all Evergreen Life Services operating units and programs." The complete Evergreen Life Services Board Governing Mission can be found in Exhibit A.

Board-savvy CEOs and their boards have put their governing missions to good use as a strategic governing framework within which the board's detailed governing responsibilities can be mapped out (for example, working out the detailed process for updating strategic directions or negotiating performance targets with the CEO and applying the targets in evaluating CEO performance). These board governing mission statements have also proved useful in orienting new board members and explaining the work of the board to the general public and key stakeholders. And many nonprofits have used their governing missions as a tool for recruiting new board members and seeking financial contributions and grants (demonstrating to these potential board members, donors, and funders that the nonprofit really does take governing seriously).

BOARD COMMITTEE STRUCTURE

Board-savvy CEOs know that well-designed board standing (sometimes called "governing") committees are one of the preeminent keys to high-impact governing performance. They enable the board to divide the highly complex and demanding work of governing into "chewable chunks," ensure thorough preparation for full board meetings, and provide board members with an opportunity to become real experts in the detailed work of governing. Well-designed committees, as I discuss in Chapter Three, can also be employed in incrementally fine-tuning the board's governing work, as what I think of as continuous board improvement vehicles.

By "well-designed," I mean committees that correspond to the actual streams of governing decisions and judgments described earlier

EXHIBIT A
EVERGREEN LIFE SERVICES BOARD
GOVERNING MISSION

The Evergreen Life Services Board of Directors, as the Evergreen corporate governing body:

- Serves as the steward and guardian of Evergreen Life Services' values, vision, and mission.

- Plays a leading, proactive role in Evergreen Life Services' strategic decision making, and in setting strong, clear strategic directions and priorities for all Evergreen Life Services operating units and programs.

- Monitors Evergreen Life Services operational performance against clearly defined performance targets.

- Ensures that the Evergreen Life Services' image and relationships with its clients, the public at large, and key stakeholders are positive and that they contribute to Evergreen Life Services' success in carrying out its mission.

- Makes sure that Evergreen Life Services possesses the financial and other resources necessary to realize its vision and carry out its mission fully.

- Ensures that the Board's composition is diverse, that its members possess the attributes and qualifications required for strong governance, and that the governing knowledge and skills of Board members are systematically developed.

- Ensures that Board members are fully engaged in the governing process and that the resources they bring to the Board are fully utilized in governing.

- Takes accountability for its own performance as a governing body, setting clear, detailed Board governing performance targets and regularly monitoring and assessing Board performance.

- Appoints a President/CEO who is responsible for providing executive direction to all Evergreen Life Services programs and administrative operations and works in close partnership with the CEO.

- Reaches agreement with the CEO on his/her position description and contract.

- Ensures that clear, detailed CEO performance targets are set and that the CEO's performance against these targets is regularly and formally evaluated.

in this chapter: strategic and operational planning; performance oversight and monitoring; external/stakeholder relations; and the board's management of itself as a governing body. Each committee should also cut across all of the nonprofit or public organization's programs, functions, and administrative units. The Evergreen Life Services Board Standing Committee Structure (Exhibit B) clearly satisfies these two key design criteria. The Evergreen Board's Board Operations Committee, by the way, is a contemporary version of the traditional executive committee. Rather than serving as a petite board that reviews all recommended actions before the full board meeting, the board operations (often called "governance") committee is responsible for coordinating the work of the board.

Basing committees on the actual work of governing could not be more different from the old-fashioned silo structure that once predominated in the world of nonprofit and public governance. Tying the board's committees to particular programmatic areas (such as education, counseling, bus services, curriculum and instruction, the annual meeting, and the like) and narrow managerial and administrative areas (such as buildings and grounds, personnel, and finance), the silo structure has bedeviled countless nonprofit and public boards in the past. For one thing, it turned board members into high-level technical advisers, focused on particular programmatic and managerial areas, and thus greatly limited the board's governing impact. For another, the focus on programmatic and managerial detail invited board micromanagement.

Finally, many nonprofit and public organizations that have created a well-designed, contemporary committee structure as part of a turning-point governing design update have also adopted guidelines to ensure that committees function as effective governing engines, ensuring that important governing issues are examined in

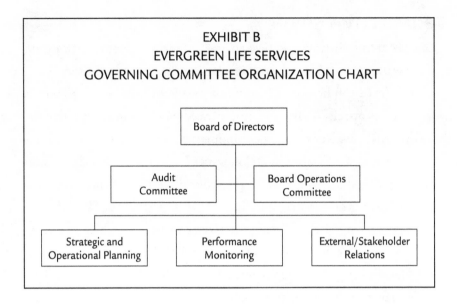

EXHIBIT B
EVERGREEN LIFE SERVICES
GOVERNING COMMITTEE ORGANIZATION CHART

Board of Directors

Audit Committee

Board Operations Committee

Strategic and Operational Planning

Performance Monitoring

External/Stakeholder Relations

detail and that recommendations are carefully crafted for full board action. Many nonprofit and public organizations also use guidelines to ensure that board members have a realistic chance of serving on more than one committee and, hence, of expanding their governing knowledge and expertise during their term on the board — a form of nonmonetary compensation for unpaid board members, as well as a source of satisfaction.

For example, the Committee Operating Guidelines that the Board of Directors of the Spokane Transit Authority adopted provide that every STA Board member "should be assigned to one (but only one) of the Governing Committees" with the exception that committee chairs also serve on the Board Operations Committee. The Guidelines also specify that "all matters coming to the full Board should go through the appropriate Governing Committee and be introduced by Committee members," and that "Governing Committee chairs and members should be rotated among Committees regularly to ensure that their governing experience is richer and more diverse."

BOARD COMPOSITION

Boards aren't abstract entities; they're essentially people making up a governing organization, and developing the people who serve on a nonprofit or public board is a major means of building the board's governing capacity. What you might call board "human resource development" involves two key components: building the board's composition and developing board members' governing knowledge and skills. Before discussing how to go about developing board composition, it's important to keep in mind that different types of boards vary widely in terms of the latitude they have in shaping their composition. Self-appointing boards, such as those of Evergreen Life Services, LifeNet, and the Miami Lighthouse for the Blind have the widest latitude, having the authority to determine the number of board seats and board member terms (typically via the bylaws) and also to fill their own vacancies. Association boards such as those of the International Economic Development Council and the International and American Associations for Dental Research have narrower latitude, since their members typically approve bylaws revisions and elect board members. And wielding the least influence are third-party-appointed boards like the Capital District Transportation Authority (appointed by the Governor of New York) and bodies elected by citizens at large, such as Wyoming's Teton County School District #1. This third type of board is typically more highly regulated than boards in the other two categories, often by state legislation spelling out how large the board will be and how vacancies will be filled.

Boards in all three categories can strengthen their composition more or less directly. All of the boards I've cited and many others have taken the first step of making their governance or board operations committee accountable for board human resource development. Many self-appointing boards like the Miami Lighthouse have taken three steps under the leadership of their governance or board operations committee to strengthen their composition.

First, they make sure there are enough seats on the board to achieve the kind of diversity that is not only symbolically and politically important (for example, in gender, race, and geographical location) but that also strengthens the process of making complex decisions (for example, experience, expertise, and vision) and can help in implementing high-stakes decisions (for example, reserving seats for representatives of key stakeholder organizations whose support is critical to success). I'm often asked by audience members and workshop participants what the ideal board size is, and I always respond by saying, first, that there's no right size, but that somewhere between fifteen and twenty-five or thirty will provide latitude for achieving diversity. And I always counsel thinking more than twice before sliding down what I think of as the slippery slope of board downsizing. Board-savvy CEOs well know that the gain in management efficiency that downsizing might produce is easily outweighed by the potential cost in terms of reduced political clout, access to resources, stakeholder representation, experience, and knowledge

Second, they develop a profile of desirable attributes and qualifications — usually brainstormed in a governance retreat, refined by the governance or board operations committee, and adopted by the full board — and use the profile to identify candidates to fill vacancies. Profiles I'm familiar with have included such elements as "visionary," "committed to our mission," "willing and able to devote the required time to governing," "successful experience on at least one other nonprofit board," and "a team player who is collaborative."

And, third, they develop and employ a detailed strategy for recruiting particular high-priority board members, such as the CEO of a key stakeholder organization. (The governance committee of the board of a health care nonprofit I worked with, for example, waged a successful campaign to convince the CEO of the community's largest hospital to join the board.)

I'm often asked in workshops about the appropriate role of the CEO in filling board vacancies, and my answer generally is "strongly supportive, but not ever the lead role." Board-savvy CEOs I've observed have, for example, made sure that their board's governance or board operations committee systematically develops and uses a detailed profile of attributes and qualifications to identify candidates and participates in campaigns to secure the commitment of really high-priority candidates. But be out front, taking the lead? Never, for two simple reasons. It's a good way to get into political trouble down the road by being too closely associated with particular board members and their issues, and it tends to reduce the board's accountability for its performance as a governing body.

Nonprofits whose boards are elected by their members, such as professional and trade associations, can develop and use a profile of board member attributes and qualifications in coming up with nominations for board seats, and even the most constrained boards, like transportation authorities and school districts, can make appointing authorities (like the governor or president of the county commission) and the electorate aware of desirable attributes and qualifications.

And all boards, no matter how their members are appointed or elected, can put in place a formal program to develop the governing knowledge and skills of their members. Many board-savvy CEOs like Jeff Finkle at IEDC, Sue Buchholtz at Evergreen Life Services, Chris Fox at IADR/AADR, and David Baumgardner at LifeNet, make sure that their board's governance or board operations committee adopts such a program, which often includes orienting new board members, making available books and articles on governing matters, and providing board members with opportunities to attend educational programs.

CHAPTER THREE

THE BOARD-SAVVY CEO AS CHIEF GOVERNING PROCESS DESIGNER

BELIEVE IT OR NOT: A TOP-TIER CEO FUNCTION

"You've got to be kidding! Mapping out process might be important at a second-or-third echelon level, but I can't see a bona fide CEO sitting at the drawing table working out who does what when, I don't care what we're talking about — strategic planning, budgeting, whatever. That's what we have staff for." I was presenting a half-day workshop for public transportation CEOs in New York State and had barely gotten into the role of the CEO as Chief Governing Process Designer, when I saw this fellow roll his eyes and up shot his hand. He definitely had a point: designing processes for getting governing work done really doesn't sound very CEO-like. It definitely doesn't conjure up the heroic CEO firing up her troops and leading them into battle. On the contrary, mapping out process sounds essentially technical, without an ounce of vision, having more to do with green eyeshades than plumed hats. You'd want to delegate it to someone on the planning staff below your planning director, right? Wrong — very wrong, as every really board-savvy CEO I've worked with would testify. In practice, meticulous attention to mapping out processes for board involvement in making governing judgments and decisions is one of the preeminent keys to high-impact governing, which is why I'm devoting a whole chapter to the CEO's role in process design.

Playing a leading role, as Chief Governing Process Designer, in helping board members figure out in detail how they should be engaged in such governing processes as leading strategic change and monitoring organizational performance is a powerful and practical way of transforming board members into productive, committed, and satisfied owners of their governing work — and, hence, stronger governing partners for the board-savvy CEO. I learned this invaluable lesson early in my career, when I was working as executive assistant and chief of staff to the president of a rapidly growing urban community college. One of my responsibilities was coordinating staff support for the college board of trustees. My boss had appointed me staff team leader for the board's planning and development committee, which had recently been created as part of a board restructuring initiative. At one of its first meetings, the president suggested that the planning and development committee oversee updating the college's values and vision statement, kicking off the process of updating the college's strategic goals.

After we spent almost an hour dealing with the *what* — coming up with definitions of values and vision and reaching agreement on the role they played in setting the college's strategic goals — we homed in on the *how* — specifically, how the planning committee and full board would be engaged in updating the values and vision statements. Now, my boss was a strong-willed chief executive who'd served as vice president for planning at a similar community college before being recruited for the presidency, so I wasn't surprised when the committee chair, who was a strong supporter and friend of my boss, just a couple of minutes into the discussion proposed that the president work with his team to come up with updated values and vision statements and bring them to the committee for review and revision, after which the committee would recommend board adoption. A less board-savvy leader might have accepted this invitation without a second thought, but my boss, an extremely board-savvy CEO, knew that following this traditional approach might result in the board's adopting the updated values and vision statements, but board members were highly unlikely to own them.

The president and I had spent a couple of hours thinking through an approach that would foster board member ownership and ego satisfaction, so he was ready for the question. But he hadn't wanted to jump the gun by supplying the answer before the question had even come up and before committee members had had an opportunity to do some brainstorming about the content of values and vision statements. He wanted them to be actively engaged before getting into process design questions, so he wouldn't be presenting his thoughts to a passive-reactive audience. By the way, his predecessor as CEO had drilled into the trustees the traditional notion that it wasn't any of their business how things got done, because their job was to focus exclusively on what should be done, leaving the how to paid staff, so my boss knew they'd feel a bit uncomfortable discussing process and didn't want to rush things. In a nutshell, what this board-savvy president recommended was that an ad hoc Values and Vision Work Group be created, consisting of the members of the planning and development committee, the president and his vice president for planning, and a faculty member and administrator from each of the three campuses.

He also recommended that this ad hoc thirteen-member body brainstorm values and vision statements in a half-day retreat, after which planning and development committee members would involve the full board in a special work session to go over the statements and come up with revisions. The chair of the Values and Vision Work Group and the president would then review the statements with focus groups on each campus, and after the Work Group used this further input to come up with a final, revised version of the values and vision statements, they would be recommended to the full board for adoption in a regular monthly board meeting. My board-savvy boss presented this process in outline form, and the trustees on the planning and development committee, once they'd gotten over their shock at being invited to discuss process, actively participated in choosing the campus faculty and administrative representatives on the Work Group and in firming up a three-month schedule for getting the job done. By the time the committee adjourned, you could tell that the trustees on the committee thought about updated values and vision statements as *their* governing products and the process for updating them as *theirs*. The energy in the room after our two-hour meeting was palpable: the tangible result of a board-savvy CEO at work as Chief Governing Process Designer.

CONTINUOUS GOVERNING IMPROVEMENT ENGINES

Chapter Two took a close look at using a retreat and a governing task force to accomplish what I called turning-point design work, putting in place a high-level statement of the board's major governing functions and outcomes — in the form of a governing mission; a structure of well-designed board standing committees that are aligned with the board's major streams of governing judgments and decisions; and a process for developing the board's composition. This chapter describes how the board-savvy CEO, playing the Chief Governing Process Designer role, can work with well-designed board standing committees — functioning as what you might call continuous governing improvement engines — to strengthen the board's governing performance by mapping out detailed processes for engaging board members in getting their work done in four key areas:

1. Board self-management

2. Strategic and operational planning/budget development

3. Performance monitoring

4. External/stakeholder relations

Keep in mind as we delve into the details of board involvement processes in these four areas that two primary goals drive the process design work that your CEO does with board committee members: (1) to strengthen the *technical capacity* of the board to make high-impact governing decisions and judgments that really do make a major, positive difference in your organization's affairs, and (2) through meaningful board involvement in making these decisions and judgments, to transform board members into *satisfied owners* of their governing work who feel strongly committed to the judgments and decisions they've been involved in making. In playing the Chief Governing Process Designer role to the hilt, the board-savvy CEO dons two hats that I will be discussing in some detail: Psychologist in Chief and Theatrical Producer.

Chapter Two examines some pretty obvious benefits of well-designed board standing committees, including making full board meetings more productive due to committee preparation and subdividing the complex, high-stakes work of governing into chewable chunks that won't choke the board to death. Board committees that are aligned with the board's governing work also make perfect continuous governing improvement partners for the CEO. Perhaps most importantly, committees provide a relatively safe venue, where the CEO and committee members can work through process details without the formality, public scrutiny, and occasional drama that tend to characterize board business meetings. By the way, even though the committee meetings of public and quasi-public boards, such as those of school districts and public transportation authorities, are typically open to the public, in practice they tend to draw few if any public spectators. The more intimate, collegial setting of a committee meeting, where by definition final decisions are not being made (that's always the full board's prerogative), means the CEO and committee members can toss around ideas without the CEO's risking the potential loss of face that can occur in full board meetings, and also without board members playing to the galleries.

Committee accountability, knowledge, and expertise are also important factors that make well-designed committees effective continuous governing improvement partners for the CEO. Being formally accountable for representing the full board in the governing area of, say, performance oversight and monitoring, makes the accountable committee infinitely more receptive to working out process questions with the CEO than the full board could ever be. And, as a committee accumulates experience in dealing with its assigned function, whether it's planning, monitoring, or external relations, it can bring considerable knowledge and expertise to bear on designing processes for board engagement.

I'll never forget what happened to a very un-board-savvy CEO I worked with a decade or so ago who tried to convince her whole board at a regular business meeting (I was a board member) to hire a strategic planning consultant to help this social service agency update its strategic plan. I really do think she expected the discussion to go smoothly, but it spun out of control in minutes, and neither I nor the handful of her other strong supporters could come to her rescue. Feeling little accountability in the area of strategic planning, bringing scant strategic planning knowledge to bear, and coming from multiple perspectives, the majority of board members picked the proposal to pieces, and a few even indulged in some public grandstanding. (One irate board member, for example, used the occasion to contribute a passionate monologue about conserving scarce dollars to "directly benefit" clients rather than throwing it away on expensive external experts.) In this public, formal setting, it was impossible to deal with such subtleties as the need for strategic planning to meet evolving client needs more fully. The predictable outcome: a humbled and embarrassed CEO without the board's go-ahead to hire a consultant. Not only was the cause of seriously needed planning set back, the CEO lost public face and, hence, credibility. To my mind, this unsavvy CEO deserved her fate. She'd set herself up for failure, so she failed.

THE OPPOSITE OF WIMPY

I'd just finished describing why standing committees were the ideal vehicles for a CEO to work with in mapping out and fine-tuning processes for board engagement in key governing areas when one of the association CEOs attending my program on building high-impact board-CEO governing teams raised a question that, to judge from his worried expression, bothered him mightily. Here's the gist of what he asked:

> OK, Doug, let's say you sit down with the board's performance monitoring committee to discuss, for example, how to strengthen both the content and format of financial reporting, and the discussion gets really detailed, like whether it would be good to use bar charts in reporting actual versus budgeted expenditures, or whether you should use a different set of cost categories for reporting expenditures — say, reporting by major operational areas rather than line items like travel. Aren't you opening Pan-

dora's box, inviting the board members on the committee to get into your business and, therefore, opening you and your staff to micromanagement? I was taught that any really strong, self-respecting CEO keeps the board's focus on the big picture, the forest — setting long-range goals, for example — and away from the trees. It sounds like you're saying, "Welcome to the trees; come on in and get involved in my and my staff's work." That seems pretty weak and dangerous to me, so you've got some more explaining to do.

My immediate, gut response was a trifle glib, in effect: I feel your pain, but welcome to the real world. More seriously, I pointed out, in the first place, that the supposed solid line — the fire wall, if you will — separating the board's forest from the CEO's and staff's trees is a highly abstract theoretical construct that always breaks down in practice and that trying to defend the line as a hard-and-fast barrier can jeopardize your CEO position and even your career. It doesn't take much thinking to understand how fallacious this traditional little golden rule for distinguishing the board's work from the CEO's and staff's work is. For example, everyone knows that the annual budget is a preeminent governing product: putting in place both annual operating goals and plans and the annual expenditure plan. It's without question one of the big kahunas of governance, deserving serious board attention. What attention exactly? When? How? Do we open the annual budget process with a retreat? How many budget work sessions does the planning committee host? And so on. The board-savvy CEO knows that board members should have a say in how they participate in such processes as annual budget preparation for three obvious reasons:

1. They are spending significant time and energy.

2. They have preferences, knowledge and experience that need to be taken into account in mapping out their role.

3. And if they don't play a role in determining precisely how they will be involved in governing areas like budget preparation, they can't be expected to feel any accountability for, or ownership of, the resulting product, be it an annual budget or a long-range plan.

Far from being seen as weak, CEOs who invite committee members to participate in process design are viewed as strong, secure leaders who aren't afraid to discuss the *how*, as well as the *what*, of governing work with committee members. I spend a lot of time interviewing board members one-on-one in preparing for retreats and other consulting engagements. Thinking about this chapter over the past weekend, I pulled out of my files interview notes from recent engagements. In one instance, the CEO had worked closely with her board's planning committee to update the board's role in the annual operational planning process, including reaching agreement on the upcoming board planning retreat that I'd been retained to facilitate.

Here are some of the responses to the question "What is it like working with Denise (the CEO)?" "She's great to work with, mainly because she really takes our input seriously." "She's open to our ideas about our role and doesn't have a defensive bone in her body." "I was stunned — and pleased — when she brainstormed with our committee on how to strengthen our board's involvement in the budget process. That would never have happened with her predecessor." "So far as I can tell, she really does want to understand our expectations about playing an important role in shaping the budget, not just thumbing through what staff have produced." I could go on, but I'm sure you get the point. This was a tremendously board-savvy CEO who'd earned the board's appreciation and respect through her collaboration in mapping out the board's involvement in one of the most critical governing processes. She'd also expanded her psychic line of credit with the board by signaling that she trusted board members not to take advantage of her invitation to get involved in process design by lapsing into micromanagement.

Don't think for a minute that CEOs who take a collaborative approach to designing processes for engaging board members in making governing judgments and decisions are in any way being weak or passive. On the contrary, board-savvy CEOs know that they've got to play a very strong and assertive role in the design process if it's to succeed. You'll never see a board-savvy CEO sitting down with, say, the board's performance monitoring committee and kicking off a process design discussion by simply asking committee members: "What ideas do you have for strengthening how you carry out your role of monitoring financial and operational performance? What's not working well, in your opinion, and what improvements do you think we should build into the monitoring process?" That kind of passive, open-ended (and incredibly dumb) question would obviously be a recipe for a chaotic meeting, as board members chimed in with a hodgepodge of ideas coming from different perspectives and drawing on different experiences and biases, and could very well end up producing a process that would warm Dr. Frankenstein's heart.

The polar opposite of a passive participant in the design process, the board-savvy CEO in her capacity as Chief Governing Process Designer meticulously prepares for the committee design session, giving considerable advance thought to how board members might be more productively engaged in a particular process and arrives at the committee design session prepared to discuss specific approaches that might get the job done. This involves a balancing act, as the board-savvy CEO decides how far to go in recommending specific steps and what blanks to leave open for board members to fill. For example, I recently sat in on a meeting of the community relations committee of a school board that had decided in a planning retreat the year before that board members should be actively involved in building a positive school district image in the community. Charged to play a leading role in this area, the external relations committee had launched a board speakers bureau, booking board members to speak in pertinent community forums such as Rotary and Lions Club luncheons.

The superintendent had prepared for the session by conducting a simple survey of board members who'd been involved thus far as presenters, asking them to assess their experience on the podium, identifying strengths and weaknesses, and to come up with some steps that might be taken to strengthen such presentations in the future. Analyzing the survey results, the superintendent prepared a briefing paper for the committee to use as a discussion guide, including a list of what appeared to be the most significant strengths and weaknesses of the speakers bureau thus far (for example, on the plus side that audience feedback had been on the whole very positive, and, on the negative, that board presenters had frequently been stumped by audience questions).

The guide also included a summary of the recommendations for improvement that board members had come up with (for example, that the superintendent or one of her associate superintendents accompany every board speaker to events to help answer audience questions and that more creative graphics be woven into the PowerPoint slides being used). The superintendent went a step further by assessing each of the recommendations in terms of potential impact and the required investment of time and money, coming up with what appeared to be the most cost-effective improvements. The discussion I witnessed was very lively and laid the foundation for a very productive follow-up session for which this highly board-savvy superintendent had prepared a set of potential action steps the committee might take.

PREPARING TO PLAY THE CHIEF GOVERNING PROCESS DESIGNER ROLE

When I was describing the Chief Governing Process Designer role in a presentation to trade association CEOs a couple of months ago, the quizzical looks on several faces and many of the questions that came up vividly brought home that this was not only unfamiliar territory but also extremely uncomfortable for many CEOs, and even threatening for some. I was reminded how different what I was describing was from the traditional role that many, if not most, CEOs played in board committee meetings: going over formal documentation (finished staff work) and garnering committee comments, explaining recommended actions and asking for committee approval, and the like — a formal, somewhat distant (though not necessarily cold or unfriendly) role conveying a definite we-they feel.

In a nutshell, the CEO's traditional job is to convince board committee members to sign off on the recommended actions before them, and if the CEO does her job well, the committee will go along. If the CEO can't get the committee to act, then she'll almost certainly lose some face. Too many of these losses can seriously erode the CEO's credibility, as many of my readers have no doubt learned. Since the role of Chief Governing Process Designer is radically different from the CEO's traditional interaction with committee members, it makes sense to think about what it takes to bring off the new, less familiar role. Experience has taught me that a four-pronged strategy is critical to becoming a successful Chief Governing Process Designer; the CEO should:

1. Make sure that committee members understand and are firmly committed to their committees' doing the process design work that's at the heart of their committees' role as continuous governing improvement vehicles.

2. Think of himself as the design consultant to the board's committees.

3. Bring substantial technical knowledge to the design process.

4. Play an active facilitator role in committee design sessions.

Wearing my board development consulting hat over the past twenty-five years, I've learned that board members often don't "get" their committees' role as continuous governance improvement vehicles, even though it's explicitly mandated in the committees' formal functional descriptions. It's so different from the traditional committee role of reviewing recommendations and reports as part of getting ready for the board business meeting that it very often doesn't penetrate board members' consciousness. That was the experience of a local nonprofit emergency medical transportation service that implemented a new board committee structure a couple of years ago. The formal functional description for every committee included the responsibility to "work closely with the Executive Director in continuously updating processes for board involvement in its area of responsibility." However, when the new committee chairs got together with the board chair and CEO to discuss the orientation program for their new committee members, everyone other than the CEO drew a blank when the process design role came up. Even the board chair, a fervent advocate for board capacity building who'd provided strong leadership for the board restructuring initiative, wasn't sure what this responsibility entailed.

Alerted to a serious potential implementation issue, the board-savvy CEO of this medical transportation nonprofit took concrete steps to ensure that the new committees did, indeed, carry out their process design responsibilities. For example, he met with the new committee chairs in a follow-up session focusing exclusively on the committees' process design mandate, working through a number of practical examples, such as updating the process for board involvement in financial performance monitoring. He made sure that the orientation program for new committee members included a thorough description of the committees' process design function with plenty of time for questions and discussion. And he worked with each committee chair in scheduling a special committee work session dedicated to process design. Thus was the responsibility institutionalized to the extent that it couldn't easily drop through the proverbial crack.

Of course, even though committee members understand and are committed to carrying out their process design responsibility, the CEO might not be prepared to play a strong supportive role. I was chatting with a tremendously board-savvy CEO a few years ago — the head of a rapidly growing international professional association — about her work with the association board's relatively new standing committees. I had worked closely with her and the governance task force in coming up with the board's new standing committee structure, and every one of the committee's functional descriptions included the responsibility for designing processes for board involvement in their respective areas. What she shared went something like this. "You, know, Doug," she confided, "even though we'd discussed this role thoroughly in our governance task force meetings and in your and my follow-up conversations, I worried more about how to help my new committees carry out this responsibility than any other of the dozens of implementation issues we had to deal with. At some point, it occurred to me that your work with the task force gave me a model: I had to think of myself as the primary design consultant to each of the committees."

What she meant was that, like any other capable consultant, she would have to figure out how to support her committee members in going through the design process themselves, and while she'd be at the table as an active participant, she had to be careful not to preempt the committee's deliberations by donning her formal CEO hat and telling them the right answers. In practice, she realized, this meant that she'd be doing a fair amount of work behind the scenes, which definitely wasn't the traditional approach she'd grown accustomed to over the years. For example, before a committee met to do process design work, she needed to huddle with the committee chair to discuss the steps committee members would need to follow in, for example, updating the board's role in fashioning annual operational priorities and goals, as a prelude to the detailed budget preparation process. Wearing her consultant hat, she also needed to familiarize herself with advances and best practices in areas in which her committees would be doing process design work. For example, as I'll discuss later in this chapter, if she was to help the board's planning committee figure out how to engage board members in leading high-stakes, complex change, she had to do in-depth research on developments in the rapidly evolving field of change management, which, by the way, has moved well beyond traditional, comprehensive strategic planning. Without an in-depth technical understanding of the field, she couldn't possibly be an effective consultant to the committee.

Facilitators don't behave like traditional CEOs, which is to say they don't plunk a document down in front of a committee, go through it explaining key points and answering questions, and then call for committee action. Instead, they guide and support committee members in working their way through a process such as designing the board's role in updating a values and vision statement, keeping the discussion on point, making sure that important technical issues that emerge are adequately discussed, and the like. They are process managers and expediters who might, indeed, have "skin in the game," but don't behave as if their role is to make sure committee members come up with the one right answer. A really capable facilitator will make sure that as many possible right answers come up as feasible and help committee members explore them adequately enough to make an informed choice. For example, there are many possible approaches to board member engagement in updating a values and vision statement — including brainstorming in a retreat, employing a task force, utilizing a number of focus groups, or a combination of two or more of these approaches. The CEO, wearing the facilitator hat, wants to make sure that the pros and cons associated with each potential approach are adequately explored by her board's planning committee before making a commitment.

DESIGNING WITH THE GOVERNANCE OR BOARD OPERATIONS COMMITTEE

In Chapter Two I describe a relatively recent innovation in nonprofit and public board structure that is rapidly replacing the traditional executive committee: a governance or board operations committee that is responsible, among other things, for coordinating and managing the work of the board. The old-time executive committee, typically comprising the board's officers, has tended to function as what I call a "petite board," reviewing and even revising actions that will be on the agenda of the upcoming board meeting — in effect, making the full board meeting a largely redundant and ceremonial affair since everything has essentially already been decided. For obvious reasons, the old-time executive committee is widely unloved and resented by the "second-class" board members who don't serve on it and are turned into a passive audience for decisions already made.

Earlier this year, I interviewed the CEO of a rapidly growing, medium-sized business who'd been recruited a year or so earlier to serve on the board of a nonprofit nursing home. When I asked him to tell me about his board experience, he responded that he was "discouraged," "feeling disgusted," and thinking about resigning. When I asked why, he explained that, drawing on his successful business experience, he'd expected to make a major contribution to the board, but that he'd found himself in board meetings spending most of the time just ratifying the decisions the board's executive committee had already made. Over the years, I've probably heard similar accounts a hundred times.

By contrast, the board operations or governance committee, which is always headed by the board chair and typically includes the chairs of the board's other standing committees and the CEO (usually as a nonvoting member), does not review beforehand the content of recommended actions going to the full board; nor does it have the power to prevent a recommendation from one of the board's standing committee from going to the full board or to revise any committees' recommendations to the board. It is truly a board coordination and management body that pays special attention to managing and updating three key governing processes: renewing and strengthening the board's composition, managing the board's governing performance, and maintaining the board-CEO working relationship. I'll address board composition and performance management in this chapter and the board-CEO relationship in Chapter Four.

In Chapter Two I describe how the board operations or governance committees of many nonprofit boards have taken important steps to strengthen their boards as a human resource, such as making sure that the board is large enough to achieve the kind of diversity that is critical to growth in today's world, developing a profile of desired board member attributes and qualifications and using it to recruit new board members, and fashioning and executing strategies to recruit particularly desirable board members, such as the CEO of a community's largest employer to serve on the regional economic development corporation. In her Chief Governing Process Designer capacity, the CEO can assist the board's governance or board operations committee in updating strategies to strengthen the board's composition, as circumstances evolve.

To take a recent example, after an intensive two-day strategic planning retreat that resulted in a strategic decision to grow clients and revenues by expanding geographically, the governance committee of a nonprofit serving persons with developmental disabilities, working closely with its CEO, came up with a recommendation to add five new board seats that would be reserved for representatives of stakeholder organizations in the geographical areas targeted for expansion. A key part of implementing this board expansion strategy was putting in place a process for identifying and assessing stakeholder organizations in order to come up with a primo list of CEOs and board chairs who might be tapped for board service. Defining a stakeholder as any organization with which it made sense to build and maintain a working relationship because significant stakes were involved (such as political support, high-level technical input, and money), the committee's assessment resulted in the identification of four preeminent stakeholders: a mayor, a hospital CEO, a chamber of commerce board chair, and the executive director of a community foundation.

The board operations committee of another nonprofit I worked with, which had made a decision to develop and pilot test two new social enterprises (profit-making entities that would generate working capital for the nonprofit), worked closely with its CEO in updating the profile of desirable board member attributes and qualifications to include "successful entrepreneurial experience." The CEO and board operations committee also put together a process for identifying and recruiting these entrepreneurs, including a significantly updated recruitment packet aimed at attracting business involvement on the board, which, among other things, clearly described what the nonprofit intended to achieve by launching social enterprises.

Turning to board performance management, I've made the point more than once that governing, by its very nature, is a collaborative function and that doing it at a high level depends on the strong leadership of the Strategic Governing Team: the board, CEO, and the CEO's top lieutenants. But board-savvy CEOs know that a critical ingredient of the kind of high-impact governing that makes a significant difference is the board's management of itself as a governing body. In my experience, boards that take clear accountability for their governing performance tend to do a more effective job of governing. Since board members are typically extremely busy people who find coming up with enough time to govern at a high level very challenging, board-savvy CEOs, in their Chief Governing Process Designer capacity, avoid getting their boards involved in elaborate performance management processes, instead relying on simple, straightforward approaches.

The natural first step is to make sure that the official functional description of the board's governance or board operations committee explicitly mentions responsibility for governing performance management. This is critical because, in my experience, individual board members are seldom willing to identify performance problems of their peers on the board, much less attempt to correct erring colleagues. This was brought home again recently when I was interviewing the board members of a community development nonprofit. When I asked one of my interviewees to tell me about the board's policing of its own governing performance, he said "nonexistent." He went on to say that a couple of his board colleagues were blowing off committee meetings, which really upset him. When I asked him if he'd tried to talk to them about missing important meetings, he just laughed, and said: "Give me a break; life's too short. I'll be seeing these guys all the time at the club, the grocery store, you name it. Let someone else be the governing cop!" By assigning responsibility to a committee, a board has "institutionalized" the performance management function, taking it out of the realm of personal relations and making it safe to be critical of underperforming board members.

The next step is to have the responsible committee develop a simple set of performance targets and standards for individual board members and, after securing full-board approval, employ these in ongoing monitoring of performance, identifying and resolving issues as they develop. Examples of real-life performance targets and standards include: not missing more than two consecutive board or committee meetings without a valid excuse; coming to board meetings having thoroughly reviewed the board packet; not directing the CEO or any other staff person to do anything or asking for information that will require a special effort to supply; speaking on behalf of the organization in specified forums; participating in the annual conference; and the like. Performance standards often include interaction guidelines as well, for example: that board members will treat each other with respect; will not speak out publicly against a decision that the board has made; and will not go around the responsible standing committee to bring an issue to the full board. In my experience, draconian corrective action (like expulsion or requesting that a member not be reappointed) is seldom required; instead, counseling of erring board members works in the great majority of cases.

The most effective governance or board operations committees schedule time to kick back at the end of every year to assess the performance of the board's standing committees in carrying out their annual goals; identify performance issues; and come up with process enhancements to address the issues during the upcoming year. For example, the board operations committee of a social service agency I worked with, having identified the lack of a standard format for standing committee reports to the full board, worked with its CEO to come up with a uniform reporting format. A key element was an executive summary form that would accompany standing committee action recommendations to the board, spelling out in no more than a page the action being recommended, the rationale for the action, the expected benefits, and the anticipated costs. To take another example, the governance committee of an international association worked with the CEO in strengthening the process they followed in developing committee meeting agendas, requiring that the executive team members assigned to work with the committees provide committee chairs with a draft agenda at least two weeks before the committee meeting, review the agenda thoroughly with the committee chair, and revise the agenda based on the chair's input.

At the top of my list of things to avoid wasting your time on in the board performance management arena are board member self-assessment instruments. I've already cautioned readers to think twice before surveying board members' opinions as a board capacity-building tool, but having seen many egregious examples over the years, I feel compelled to make the point again. Board-savvy CEOs know enough to counsel their board's governance or board operations committee not to get board members embroiled in evaluating their own performance via some kind of pseudoscientific questionnaire. Although they might seem like a pretty precise measurement tool (what with their five-point numerical ranking scale for each question), these self-assessment questionnaires typically generate lots of subjective opinion that can't be put to practical use in strengthening board performance.

I vividly recall printing out ten pages of survey results that'd been e-mailed to me to help me prepare for the board governance retreat of a state association of real estate brokers around five years ago. As I thumbed through the tabulated results, I was appalled by so much time being spent generating information of so little practical value. For example, learning that 80 percent of the board members felt "very satisfied" that the board was "appropriately" involved in making strategic decisions told me absolutely nothing of value about the technical quality of the nonprofit's strategic planning process or of the strategies it was generating.

In fact, over the course of a number of one-on-one telephone interviews with board members, I learned that the outdated approach to strategic planning that the majority of board members found so satisfactory was essentially just describing what the nonprofit was already doing without generating any significant innovation. What the self-assessment results did tell me was how board members felt about one aspect of governance or another, which was interesting but of minor value in building the board's governing capacity. And it's pretty ironic that one of the functions they found most satisfying — strategic planning — was patently ineffective in generating the kind of innovation that would fuel growth in a rapidly changing, terribly challenging world. In this case, the opinion of a happy and satisfied majority was potentially dangerous since it might have prevented the nonprofit from figuring out a way to generate innovative growth initiatives.

What is the appropriate role of the CEO in the board performance management process? As with the process of filling board vacancies, the board-savvy CEO, wearing the Chief Governing Process Designer hat, can help the board's governance or board operations committee map out processes for managing and strengthening board performance and help them implement the process. Be supportive, help the governance or board operations committee do its job, but never take the lead. Board-savvy CEOs are well aware that putting on the Chief Board Disciplinarian hat would be a high-risk strategy.

DESIGNING WITH THE PLANNING COMMITTEE

Planning is a broad and tremendously powerful decision-making stream in terms of its impact on a nonprofit or public organization's directions — from updating organizational values and vision, setting long-range goals, and generating change initiatives to deal with high-stakes out-of-the-box issues at the strategic end of the spectrum to the more pedestrian planning functions of updating next year's program goals and the line-item budget. So it makes the best of sense for the CEO to work closely with her board's planning committee in mapping out processes for board involvement in making planning decisions that are not only informed, rational and technically sound but that also foster board ownership and commitment. And in our complex and rapidly changing world, as board-savvy CEOs well know, no planning process deserves as much board attention as what I call "out-of-the-box" change-focused planning, which, in my professional opinion, is the gold standard for board involvement, for four primary reasons:

1. The stakes are tremendously high, because in today's highly complex and rapidly changing environment, standing pat and failing to come up with major change initiatives to capitalize on growth opportunities and counter negative trends is a sure recipe for decline, and for some nonprofits, even extinction.

2. The work of generating significant change initiatives to deal with out-of-the-box issues is extremely challenging and exciting, unlike the more routine process of updating an annual budget.

3. The experience, expertise, and diverse perspectives of board members make them a precious asset in nonroutine, change-focused planning, particularly if the board is highly diverse. In fact, diversity is such an asset in change-focused planning that it has led many nonprofit boards to recruit new members who bring more experience and expertise to the planning process, and even to enlarge their boards in the interest of greater diversity.

4. And really board-savvy CEOs know that, as a consequence of the foregoing three factors, they can't afford *not* to engage their board actively in change-focused planning, and that they've got no choice but to work closely with the board's planning committee in mapping out the process for board engagement. Otherwise, they stand a good chance of being saddled with the kind of bored, underemployed, and disgruntled board members who will inevitably blame the CEO for their being left out of the significant action.

It's appropriate at this point to say a bit about the change-focused, out-of-the-box planning process. It has rapidly been supplanting traditional comprehensive long-range planning, which has proved to be a more effective tool for refining and projecting into the future what an organization is already doing rather than for generating significant innovation and change. In the first place, out-of-the-box planning is driven by the identification of out-of-the-box issues and the selection of the issues that will be dealt with now — this year — not five years in the future. In my book *Leading Out-of-the-Box Change: The Chief Executive's Essential Guide to Achieving Nonprofit Innovation and Growth* (Governance Edge, 2012), I define out-of-the-box issues as "opportunities to grow and challenges and threats standing in the way of growth — that cannot be effectively handled by the annual operational planning/ budget preparation process because of their technical and/or political complexity and the amount of risk involved." The second key feature of this new approach to generating significant organizational change is the fashioning of detailed projects, what I call "change initiatives," to address the issues that have been selected, which can relate to a wide range of factors, such as evolving client/customer need, organizational leadership, internal culture, and image/stakeholder relations.

An international association I worked with a few years ago provides an excellent example of successful out-of-the-box change planning, employing a carefully designed process that the board-savvy CEO worked out with the board's planning and development committee. The impetus for launching the process was a CEO who recognized that ominous trends — such as consolidation in the industry the association represented, declining attendance at the association's annual conference and stand-alone educational programs, and growing board members' frustration with their generally passive-reactive governing role — couldn't be effectively handled by the business-as-usual planning process that the association had been using. In preparation for a critical planning process discussion with the planning and development committee that'd been scheduled a month hence, the CEO took the trouble to educate himself on important developments in the fields of planning and change management. So he arrived at the meeting with a firm grasp of current thinking about how to identify and address opportunities and challenges that don't fit in the box. I'll briefly describe the key elements of the process that resulted from this CEO's design collaboration with his planning and development committee.

At the daylong board-CEO-executive team planning retreat that kicked off the new planning process, breakout groups led by board members analyzed major environmental conditions and trends, identified issues (both opportunities and challenges) emerging from the environmental analysis, assessed issues in terms of the potential cost to the association of *not* taking action to deal with them in the near term, and brainstormed possible change initiatives. The day opened with members of the planning and development committee briefing their colleagues on trends and conditions, using an attractive set of PowerPoint slides, which certainly strengthened the committee's ownership of the process, as did the early involvement of all board members and the use of board members to lead breakout groups. By the end of the day, several board members had become ardent change champions, and the majority had clearly bought into the process.

The retreat facilitator analyzed the content that had been generated and provided the CEO and executive team with his best thinking about the out-of-the-box issues that deserved attention, which the executive team used in coming up with the issues that it recommended to the planning and development committee: significant board frustration with their governing role and structure; the need to stem the decline of attendance at the annual conference and educational programs; and the opportunity to expand internationally. After a thorough discussion, the planning and development committee selected these three issues and got full board concurrence at the next meeting.

Three change-planning vehicles were then launched: a Governance Task Force consisting of seven of the twenty-five board members; an Educational Program Work Group consisting of both association executive team members and nonboard volunteers; and an International Growth Task Force also consisting of executives and volunteers. Working under the direction of the planning and development committee, which closely monitored progress, these three issue-focused bodies fashioned a number of concrete change initiatives that were ultimately adopted by the full board.

Not only did a well-crafted planning process result in the development of a set of concrete change initiatives in a relatively short period of time, but early, meaningful involvement of all board members, along with the intensive involvement of the board's planning and development committee, ensured the strong board support that was necessary to get the initiatives implemented, despite the normal and predictable resistance of several staff members who, like most human beings, would have been happier not to have had to change.

Supported by board-savvy CEOs, nonprofit and public organizations continuously implement less dramatic planning process improvements that produce substantial benefits while requiring much less change than the real-life association example described above. The board planning committees of many nonprofits I've worked with have strengthened their annual operational planning and budget preparation process through such incremental tweaking as:

- adding to the process a front-end operational issue identification and analysis component aimed at focusing the board's attention on major issues that should be addressed in detailed budget preparation;

- instituting a series of board budget work sessions during the preparation process hosted by the planning committee, aimed at eliciting board guidance at key points in the process on such issues as anticipated significant new expenditures and the institution of a new salary schedule; and

- revising the final budget document to make it a more effective public education tool by adding an operational priorities and goals component and more clearly describing the organization's operating units and programs.

DESIGNING WITH THE PERFORMANCE MONITORING COMMITTEE

The time was three years ago; the place was the boardroom of a regional public transportation authority; the occasion was the monthly board business meeting. I could tell that the new chair of the board's performance oversight and monitoring committee was a bit nervous when she stood up at the board meeting, remote in hand, to present the monthly operating performance report, and I, sitting in the audience, was feeling more than a little apprehensive myself. You see, this was a real first in the authority's history. Traditionally, the authority's chief financial officer presented the performance report — dealing with such matters as ridership numbers, on-time performance, equipment repair, and capital project status — typically by thumbing through the weighty document that board members received a week before the meeting and pointing out what appeared to be significant items. Board members tended to doze off through the presentations, until the speaker noted a dramatic development like a major cost overrun or fatal accident.

As if the committee chair presenting the report wasn't enough of a change, she used PowerPoint slides that highlighted key performance indicators rather than walking board members through a thick document. Of course, the traditional document had gone out to board members the week before as it always had; eliminating it at this early point would have caused a needless stir. Even if they didn't pore over it, some board members treated the document as a kind of security blanket — if I need it, it's there. And the CFO was seated next to the committee chair, prepared to answer any thorny questions that might come up (two or three did). All in all, it was a successful experiment, upgrading performance reporting and empowering the board's performance oversight and monitoring committee.

There were a couple of ancillary benefits as well. Since board meetings were well attended and televised, members of the general public got the message loudly and clearly that this board was in the driver's seat, rather than merely being led around by the nose by the CEO and his staff. And the committee chair's relationship with, and support for, the CEO and his top lieutenants were without question strengthened by her ego-satisfying experience. When we'd discussed making the change in a committee meeting a couple of months earlier, she'd been notably unenthusiastic, making a big point of her lack of technical knowledge and experience. "I don't relish the thought of being embarrassed in public by not being able to answer questions," I recall her saying. She was clearly euphoric when I chatted with her after the board meeting, and she must have mentioned how much she appreciated the staff support she'd received at least three times. As a matter of fact the CEO and his CFO had been tremendously supportive, including staging a couple of rehearsal sessions with the executive team, where the committee chair was able to run through the slide show and answer questions, so she was reasonably comfortable presenting the report at the board meeting once she got into it.

This was a pretty dramatic example of the power of creative process design in the area of board performance monitoring, but I've worked with a number of board-savvy CEOs over the years who have teamed up with their board's monitoring committees in coming up with less dramatic process tweaks aimed at enhancing both board oversight and ownership. For example, over the course of a two-hour work session a year or so ago, the CEO and board monitoring committee of a local children's services nonprofit with multiple locations around the county came up with two creative tweaks that certainly added richness to what could easily be a pretty sterile oversight function. They instituted a schedule of committee member visits to particular sites, at which staff members briefed the visitors on their operation and conducted a guided tour, and they also implemented a schedule of quarterly in-depth committee assessments of particular services, including a special report to the full board after every assessment.

Harking back to the true story that opened this section — about a dramatic new approach to reporting operating performance to the board of a transportation authority — I'll close by reminding the reader that board members don't necessarily welcome the opportunity to play more of a leading and public role in reporting to their board colleagues, primarily, so far as I can tell, because they're not comfortable with the technical content of what they're to present and afraid of looking inept or foolish in public. But the board-savvy CEO, knowing the benefits in terms of board member feelings of satisfaction and ownership, won't take no for an answer. Experience has taught me that if the CEO adds to her persistence strong encouragement, the promise of strong staff support, and the guarantee that it will go well, the great majority of board members will step up to the plate, even if grudgingly. And when a fearful board member ends up succeeding at something he thought he wasn't able to do, as a result of CEO encouragement and assistance, you'd better believe that the CEO's line of credit with that board member has grown significantly.

DESIGNING WITH THE EXTERNAL RELATIONS COMMITTEE

Faced with the challenge of convincing voters to renew a one-quarter cent real estate tax levy to support district operations, the superintendent and external relations committee of a school board I worked with a decade ago collaborated in designing a detailed process for building community support. The strategy the committee came up with included booking board members — armed with pertinent facts and creative visual aids — to speak in various forums on behalf of the levy, putting together a blue ribbon citizens' committee to raise money to pay for levy advertising, and arranging for the board chair and superintendent to meet with the editorial board of the local newspaper and to appear on morning talk shows. The external relations committee and superintendent also orchestrated meetings of the whole school board with the city council, county commission, and community college board of trustees to secure levy endorsements.

As I discussed in Chapter Two, this is a good example of engaging board members in doing nongoverning work. Other examples of important nongoverning work that board members are often engaged in are fund-raising, testifying on behalf of your nonprofit at a state legislative committee meeting, attending public events on behalf of the board, such as a graduation exercise, and taking responsibility for maintaining contacts with key stakeholder organizations. The danger, as I pointed out earlier, is that nongoverning work, which can be more fun and ego satisfying than the hard work of making governing decisions and judgments, can get out of hand, detracting from the board's preeminent job: governing. Of course, not every nonprofit or public organization is so dependent on public opinion and support that it needs a board external relations committee. But when board involvement in external relations is clearly called for — as in the case of a school district dependent on passing tax levies — then it makes sense to have a standing committee map out processes for board engagement that will help to ensure that board members aren't overextended to the detriment of their core governing mission.

CHAPTER FOUR

THE BOARD-SAVVY CEO AS CHIEF GOVERNING RELATIONSHIP MANAGER

LESSONS FROM THE FIELD

The reader might recall the true story in Chapter One about "Howard," whose board — despite his mastery of such critical technical functions as strategic and financial planning that are at the heart of CEOship and the fact that things were going quite well, organizationally speaking — parted company with him. The primary reason, apparently, was Howard's failure to take steps to engage his board members in a meaningful fashion in shaping governing decisions. In effect, Howard had been treating his board as an audience for very capably crafted staff work, and, not being satisfied owners of their governing work, board members had found it easy to send him packing. Talking with the chair and other board officers after Howard's departure, I learned that the sundered tie between Howard and his board wasn't the result of inadequate board engagement alone. Howard had also obviously paid scant attention to keeping his working relationship with the board in good repair.

As the board chair observed over lunch one day, Howard "didn't really give much of a damn about the people side of the business," going on to say that Howard had treated the board like a kind of a governing machine "that would just keep humming along if he fueled it with good staff work." "He basically took us for granted," according to the chair, "and we really resented it." Looking back, I feel pretty certain that if Howard had been a more skillful and dedicated relationship manager, he would have earned the time he needed to help his board become more engaged. But it was, sadly, too late.

Howard's experience taught me a valuable lesson early in my consulting career, and it's been drummed into me over and over again in the quarter century since we worked together. Indeed, if a CEO's professional expertise and satisfactory — even stellar — organizational performance were sufficient to keep board-CEO working relationships close, positive, and enduring, I wouldn't be writing this book. Since working with Howard and his board I've seen so many seriously eroded board-CEO partnerships, even though the nonprofit or public organization is achieving its goals, things are going smoothly, and the CEO is a master of his trade, that I've considered handing out bumper stickers that say "It's all about the relationship, stupid!"

As I write this chapter, I'm reminded of a more recent case in point that had a happier ending than Howard's. On the watch of its extraordinarily bright and dedicated president and CEO — let's call her "Carol"— this rapidly growing international professional association was a success story by any measure: launching innovative new programs, growing its membership and revenues, and expanding at a rapid clip worldwide. Carol had become a superstar in her field. Naturally, she traveled continuously in her job, mainly visiting chapters, and she was also a tremendously respected, highly visible volunteer in related professional associations that she believed would strengthen her own association. In light of Carol's obvious success as a CEO, when I began my one-on-one interviews with the board chair and other officers in preparation for the upcoming retreat I'd been retained to facilitate, I naturally expected an enthusiastically positive response to a question I always ask: How would you characterize the board's working relationship with Carol? I assumed they'd praise her to the heavens.

I was wrong! Here are some initial responses from my interview notes: "It could be worse." "I'm not exactly sure." "Not bad, no serious problems that I can tell." "It doesn't seem to be high on her list." Taken aback, I probed a bit, but couldn't pin down any specific relationship problems — just a disquieting coolness and distance. Fortunately, our upcoming retreat gave us an opportunity to do some relationship mending, which, as it turned out, did the trick. The breakout group assigned to examine the board-CEO partnership and come up with practical ideas for keeping it healthy determined, early in its deliberations, that Carol wasn't really paying much attention to her relationship with the board, leaving many board members feeling like second-class citizens. I'm happy to report that Carol, an avid lifelong learner, listened, understood, and acted. A precious working relationship was preserved and, over the next year, considerably strengthened.

MEETING THE RELATIONSHIP CHALLENGE

Keeping the board-CEO working relationship on an even keel and healthy over the long run is a major challenge. Just the fact that strong-willed people with robust egos have to be melded into enough of a team to do the extremely complex and demanding work of governing is challenging enough, but as I point out in Chapter One, other factors help to make the board-CEO partnership inherently fragile and prone to erode quickly if not diligently managed. For one thing, the high-pressure atmosphere at the top of an organization, where high-stakes and often tremendously thorny issues are addressed —

frequently with intense public scrutiny — tends to fray the board-CEO partnership. And interpersonal dynamics can take a real toll. For example, the members of boards that are appointed by third parties, such as the mayor or chair of the county commission, or elected by the general public, are often more beholden to constituencies than to the board itself and notoriously difficult to meld into a cohesive governing team. And I've run into several boards over the years whose members are significantly outranked — professionally and in terms of compensation — by the CEO, often contributing to corrosive envy on the part of board members.

Board-savvy CEOs well know that they've got to take the lead in meeting the board-CEO relationship challenge. It might theoretically be a shared responsibility, but the reality is that being unpaid volunteers who have enough of a challenge mustering the time and energy to do a bang-up governing job, board members can't be expected to take the lead in managing the working relationship with their CEO. The great majority of board members I've worked with over the years have recognized that keeping the board-CEO partnership healthy is a high priority, and they've been willing to serve on a committee charged with overseeing the partnership, but they typically expect the CEO to play the role of Chief Governing Relationship Manager.

To be sure, the average board member would probably lose some sleep over a souring relationship, knowing that it would negatively impact both governance and organizational performance. But they'd expect the CEO to take the lead in figuring out exactly what the relationship problems are and to take the initiative in fixing them, and they'd be highly unlikely to blame themselves for a failed relationship. As board-savvy CEOs well know, it's the CEO who inevitably takes the blame for relationship problems, and if the board-CEO partnership breaks down completely, the board will fire the CEO, not itself.

If this has read like a litany of bad news, the reader can take heart. The following pages describe a number of very practical, thoroughly tested strategies that nonprofit and public boards and their CEOs can employ to ensure the kind of close, positive, and enduring board-CEO partnership that is essential for high-impact governing. What's required for success is a board-savvy CEO ready and willing to play the role of Chief Governing Relationship Manager and a board that's both committed to a healthy relationship with its CEO and willing to work closely with its CEO in maintaining the relationship. This chapter focuses on five critical relationship maintenance strategies that the board-savvy CEO, in her capacity as Chief Governing Relationship Manager, can employ in collaboration with her board:

1. Make maintaining a healthy board-CEO partnership a formal board priority and function and make sure that the responsibility for overseeing maintenance of the board-CEO partnership is explicitly, formally assigned to a board standing committee — governance or board operations — headed by the board chair and consisting of the chairs of the other board standing committees and the CEO.

2. Under the leadership of the governance or board operations committee, establish and implement detailed guidelines for board-CEO and board-executive team communication and interaction.

3. Pay special attention to building strong working relationships between the board chair and CEO and between each of the board's committee chairs and the CEO.

4. Implement a well-designed process for regular, formal board evaluation of CEO performance.

5.   Employ extensive informal board-CEO and board-executive team interaction as a bonding mechanism.

A BOARD HOME FOR RELATIONSHIP MANAGEMENT

Early in my consulting career, I learned a valuable lesson about the potential cost of not building into a nonprofit or public board's structure formal accountability for managing the board-CEO working relationship. I was working with the extremely capable CEO of a midsized public transportation authority that provided bus and commuter rail services. She was in many respects a superstar, having shaped up what was a seriously leaking and off-course ship during her first three years on the job, responding to the emphatic direction of the board's executive committee. On her watch several top managers had been replaced with far more qualified successors, a modern financial management system had been installed, rigorous budget control had been instituted to end chronic overruns, and on-time performance had significantly improved. Being aware of what she'd achieved over the past five years, I began my consulting assignment with the authority confidant that one of the issues I wouldn't face was having to repair an eroded board-CEO relationship.

However, over the course of interviewing all board members early in my consulting engagement, I discovered a high degree of frustration with the CEO's leadership that was centered on her leadership priorities. Almost to a person in my interviews, board members talked about the fact that times had changed since the CEO had taken the helm: the operation was running smoothly — which everyone gave her ample credit for — and now was the time to work on the authority's image and relationships with key stakeholders, such as the state department of transportation and, at the local level, the mayor's office, county commission, chamber of commerce, and the local economic development commission. Friend building was a tremendous concern of the board members I interviewed, and they strongly felt that their CEO was still basically being, as one board member put it, "Ms. insider nuts-and-bolts manager" and neglecting her critical external diplomatic role.

Having uncovered an issue that clearly jeopardized my client board's relationship with its CEO, I naturally made an effort to ferret out how this could have happened. What I discovered was a simple but surprising explanation: the board and its CEO had never talked formally, in detail, about board members' evolving expectations about their CEO's leadership priorities. The reason? There was no formal home for such a dialogue. Concerns had been raised at various times by different board members, but always individually and never strongly enough to penetrate the consciousness of a strong-willed, hard-driving CEO who relished being an operational virtuoso. This story has a happy ending, I'm pleased to report. Not only did we have a very productive discussion about the issue at a special board-CEO work session that I facilitated, more importantly we created a new board operations committee that was explicitly charged with managing the board's relationship with its CEO. At its first meeting, the committee negotiated a new set of leadership priorities with its CEO, who made a firm commitment to begin active friend building at the state and local level.

Since those early days in my consulting career, I've seen an increasing number of nonprofit and public boards recognize that they can't afford to let their relationship with the CEO erode because of the tremendous potential cost in terms of internal management turmoil and damaged morale, a tarnished public reputation, and the expense of finding a successor. Consequently, many boards have taken two concrete steps to keep this precious relationship healthy: first, they make it a formal board priority, and second, they assign detailed management of the relationship to a particular board committee. For example, one of the formal governing functions enumerated in the Board Governing Mission of the International and American Associations for Dental Research is to work "in close partnership" with their CEO, and, like many other nonprofit and public boards, the IADR/AADR boards established a Board Operations Committee whose formal functional description includes responsibility "for the maintenance and development of the Board-Executive Director working relationship."

Assigning responsibility for overseeing and managing the board-CEO working relationship to a mainline board standing committee is perhaps the surest way to ensure that potentially damaging relationship issues aren't allowed to fall through the cracks. And because the board operations or governance committee is typically headed by the board chair and includes the chairs of the board's other standing committees (such as planning and performance monitoring) and sometimes other board officers, such as the secretary and treasurer, they are an ideal body to pay close attention to such a high-stakes, notoriously fragile relationship that can easily erode if not meticulously managed. Not only does the composition of the board operations or governance committee signal that the board-CEO relationship is a high governing priority, it also lends credibility to any agreements reached with the CEO that normally require full board approval, such as the CEO's annual leadership priorities and action to address a serious relationship issue.

Bringing this discussion to a close on a high note, I'll share two recent examples of board governance committees delivering on their promise as high-level relationship managers. Both of these true accounts illustrate how effective governance or board operations committees can be in preventing serious board-CEO relationship issues from ever developing. In one case, the CEO of an international trade association, having received his board's go-ahead to pursue a high-stakes merger with a related association, in response to ongoing consolidation in the industry that was shrinking membership and revenue, sat down with his governance committee to discuss how his focus on the merger would alter his CEO leadership priorities. They rightly feared that if he merely plowed ahead on the merger road, other CEO priorities might be dropped, causing a relationship issue. Rather than have this happen, the CEO and his board's governance committee took preemptive action: identifying a couple of other CEO priorities (such as overhauling the delivery of educational programs and traveling around to various state chapters, wearing his diplomatic hat) that could be put on hold until the merger had been consummated.

In the second instance, the CEO of a local economic development corporation who'd played a leading role, working closely with her board chair, in revitalizing her board — updating its governing role, beefing up its composition, and putting new standing committees in place — was asked by the chair of the state economic development association board to chair the board's new governance task force. Expecting that this would be a fairly routine volunteer assignment that clearly fell within her job description, the CEO hadn't done more than mention it in passing to her board in her monthly CEO update. Two months into the task force effort, however, the CEO realized that the job was going to demand much more time and travel than she'd anticipated, so she put the volunteer assignment on the agenda of the upcoming governance committee meeting, where they discussed it thoroughly. Agreeing that her involvement at the state level would pay dividends for their nonprofit over the long run, governance committee members gave her the go-ahead to continue spending time on the state task force. And she made a commitment to alert the governance committee when her volunteer involvement appeared to impinge on other CEO priorities so that they could work out a solution before a serious issue developed.

INTERACTION AND COMMUNICATION GUIDELINES

I'll begin this discussion with a couple of true tales of woe. "He's driving me crazy. Someone's got to get him in line, but I can't imagine myself doing it. Help!" I'm paraphrasing what I heard in my first interview with the executive director of a very well-regarded aging services nonprofit that operated a top-quality nursing home and assisted living facility. This CEO went on to tell me a horror story that'd begun on an auspicious note. He and his board chair had been delighted when they'd succeeded in attracting a retired senior banking executive — I'll call him "Kevin" — to the board. It hadn't been easy to convince Kevin to join a new board since he was already serving on two other boards that were taking up considerable time, but the executive director and his board chair teamed up to make a compelling case. In order to carry out the nonprofit's ambitious expansion strategy, including securing financing for a new state-of-the-art facility, they badly needed Kevin's financial acumen and rich experience. He'd be the most financially savvy board member, without question, they'd told Kevin, so there was no question he'd make a difference. How could Kevin refuse such an offer?

As I listened to this classic horror story unfold, I was reminded of the adage "Be careful what you ask for; it might come true." Early in Kevin's first week on the governing job, the executive director had a pretty clear indication that they might have opened Pandora's box. Kevin appeared at the CEO's door at 7:30 a.m. Tuesday that week, without an appointment, asking if they could chat for a few minutes. Sitting down, he explained to the executive director that since he'd be spending a good deal of time on the financing strategy for the new facility, it'd make sense for him to spend a few hours every week at headquarters, if the executive could come up with a small office. In fact, he pointed out, he'd noticed a small conference room down the hall that'd be perfect, assuming the executive director could spare it. Caught off guard, the executive director agreed, and it didn't take long for things to go downhill from there.

Settling into his new little office the next Friday, two weeks before his first board meeting, Kevin got to work with a vengeance, summoning the chief financial officer to his office to run over the financial documentation he'd need before noon to get started with his analysis of the financing requirements for the new facility. For the next three weeks, the CFO spent hours in Kevin's office, going over figures, answering questions and, eventually, producing documentation at Kevin's direction. The last straw was when the CFO missed a critical executive team meeting because he was closeted with Kevin. The executive director knew he couldn't allow the situation to continue, so he called the board chair to discuss the unfolding nightmare and decide how to handle it.

A different but similar situation had developed in a school district I worked with a few years ago. A new board member — let's call her "Melinda" — not long after her election began to visit elementary schools in the district, always arriving at the principal's office unannounced to chat about how things were going, what problems they were experiencing that she should know about, and how the board might help in solving them. Melinda also did some probing about the superintendent-principal working relationship, asking whether there were any issues she and her colleagues on the board should be aware of. Of course, the superintendent quickly heard about these visits, but she didn't want to do any red flagging without thinking the matter through. If she'd been tempted to wait, she was forced to act when she got a call one afternoon that Melinda had appeared in an elementary classroom one morning with no warning, sat in the back observing for a couple of hours, and stuck around until the lunch break to ask the teacher some questions about teaching methodology.

Both CEOs — the executive director and superintendent — understood that the unhealthy situations that'd developed in their organizations were due to the absence of guidelines to govern board member interaction with staff. They were both board savvy enough, fortunately, to recognize that they couldn't safely take on the job of disciplining their erring board members, and they needed to help their boards assume the self-policing function. The solutions were similar. In the case of the aging serving nonprofit, a previously scheduled board governance retreat provided the perfect opportunity. Working closely behind the scenes with the board chair, who chaired the committee responsible for retreat planning — board operations — the executive director came up with a retreat agenda that included a breakout group charged to brainstorm a set of guidelines for board-staff interaction that would be finalized by the board operations committee subsequent to the retreat and formally adopted by the board. Three of the guidelines that were adopted and that pretty quickly ended Kevin's ill-advised executive career provided that:

- Only the Board of Directors collectively may provide direction to the Executive Director, and only to the Executive Director.

- Neither the Board of Directors as a whole nor an individual board member may provide direction to any staff member under the Executive Director.

- Individual Board members may request information from the Executive Director or executives reporting to the Executive Director, provided that: (1) the information is easily accessible and does not require more than a few minutes to obtain for the requesting board member, and (2) the Executive Director is formally notified by the board member requesting information from one of his executive team members, and, via the Executive Director, the full Board.

The case of the erring school board member who was wandering around elementary school buildings was addressed slightly differently. Since there wasn't a retreat on the board's agenda, the school board president, having been briefed by the superintendent, called a special work session of the board's governance committee to flesh out a set of interaction guidelines that were soon thereafter formally adopted by the school board. The guidelines, which were very similar to the ones adopted by the aging services nonprofit, included this proviso: "School Board members are encouraged to visit school buildings in the district, but such visits shall be arranged through the Office of the Superintendent, which will ensure that such visits do not unduly inconvenience building administrators and faculty or disrupt classroom activities."

By the way, in both cases the boards, along with their CEOs and senior executives, engaged in a robust discussion of the need for, and content of, the guidelines — in the governance retreat of the aging services nonprofit and in the special work session of the school board's governance committee. It was definitely not a case of board members' reacting to detailed recommendations from their chief executives, who were savvy enough to know that board ownership would be critical to enforcing guidelines. And Kevin and Melinda — the erring board members? Neither was explicitly mentioned during the process of working out the guidelines as the precipitating factor. Rather, to make sure they got the message loudly and clearly that continuing their aberrant behavior would violate the boards' new guidelines, they were privately counseled by their board chairs, who had no desire to embarrass their two board colleagues.

While board-CEO (and staff) interaction guidelines create boundaries that help to avert the development of issues that can erode a chief executive's working relationship with her board, communication guidelines serve as an adhesive, strengthening the board-CEO bond and making it more resistant to erosion. Board-savvy CEOs, knowing how important communication can be in strengthening their relationship with their board, explicitly map out communication guidelines with the board's governance or board operations committee. Here are three examples of guidelines that have worked well in practice:

1. The board-savvy CEO makes sure that board members are never caught off guard and embarrassed publicly by important events they're unaware of. The CEO makes sure that they are always "in the know." I'll never forget a board member's quivering with indignation when, during a board retreat, she told her colleagues about being accosted in the supermarket line by a constituent who was irate about the transit authority's changing the schedule on one of the bus lines. "I felt like an idiot," I recall this board member saying. "How could this happen without my knowing?"

2. The board-savvy CEO pays close attention to regular, formal communication with her board. For example, the president and CEO of an international trade association sends his board a biweekly e-update on major developments not only within the association (including its chapters), but also in the wider industry. And this

same CEO carefully crafts his oral presentation at quarterly board meetings, making sure that board members are apprised of his activities as CEO, including dealing with key stakeholders, knowing that board members need to have a firm grasp of his CEO leadership priorities.

3. The board-savvy CEO knows that informal communication helps to cement her relationship with board members, so meeting one-on-one with board members, say, once a quarter, often over a meal, is a tried-and-true strategy. Of course, in the case of statewide, national and international associations, this isn't really feasible, so board-savvy association CEOs rely on the telephone rather than in-person meetings.

A SOLID BOARD CHAIR-CEO ALLIANCE

The board chair, a prominent physician, and the executive director of a nonprofit clinic providing free medical and dental services to low-income community residents teamed up to brief the county commissioners on the clinic's accomplishments and financial situation and to request that the commissioners renew and increase the county's annual subsidy. A seasoned presenter, the board chair did a great job of making the case, aided by a set of talking points and PowerPoint slides the executive director had put together. Between the two of them, the chair and CEO very adroitly handled commissioners' questions and managed not only to get the subsidy renewed but also obtained a 10 percent increase. The board-savvy executive director had known that his chair's enthusiastic public advocacy on behalf of the clinic would be critical in the throes of a deep national recession that had taken its toll in the county, so he made sure that the two of them were sharing the podium at the commission meeting.

When the CEO of a national professional association began to talk with her board chair about the need for board capacity building, she realized she had a pretty rough row to hoe. Her chair was preoccupied with his pet leadership target — putting in place a detailed strategy for international growth as a way to address slow and sure decline in both members and revenues on the domestic front. And not only was he initially unconvinced that a board development initiative made sense at this point in time, he was keenly aware that three or four important board members were likely to oppose any capacity-building effort, for a purely selfish reason: fear of losing the influence they'd built up over the years. The board-savvy CEO persevered, finally convincing her chair that a more fully developed governing board would be critical to successfully implementing an international expansion effort and that his being a vocal champion for board development would be essential to overcoming resistance. So donning the change champion hat, the board chair appointed a governance task force charged to come up with recommendations to strengthen the board's role and structure, and six months later the task force recommendations were adopted unanimously. Of course, the board-savvy CEO worked closely with the chair in coming up with the right task force composition, drafting the chair's charge to the task force, convincing the chair to head the task force, and ensuring that it was well staffed.

When the board-savvy general manager (CEO) of the regional transit authority approached his board chair about the need for a better-designed process for board evaluation of his performance, suggesting that the board's governance committee devote a couple of work sessions coming up with a new approach, he got the gut response he'd expected: "If it ain't broke, why bother trying to fix it? We've got plenty going on already." No one on the board was pressuring him to improve the process, the chair pointed out; in fact, every-one seemed pretty satisfied with the questionnaire they'd been using for a decade or so. The GM didn't press the point at first, instead opting to educate his chair over the next few weeks. They were early in the new fiscal year, so there was time to redesign the process and actually use it at the end of the year. So over the course of a series of breakfast meetings, the GM convinced his chair that the current process, involving a questionnaire that essentially measured board members' opinions about the GM's functional competence in areas like financial planning and supervision, was dangerously subjective, missing the key outcomes piece and leaving both the board and GM at a disadvantage.

The next steps were for the chair and GM to reach agreement on the outline of a more outcomes-focused process and on the chair's playing the leading role in fleshing out the outline with the governance committee over the course of two work sessions, which the chair agreed to schedule. Naturally, the chair suggested that the GM, being the CEO and having a big stake in the outcome, take the lead in the work sessions, but he came around when the GM pointed out that it'd take the chair's influence to overcome the inevitable resistance from committee members who were pretty comfortable with the way evaluation had been done for as long as they'd been on the board. As the GM expected, the board chair's strong leadership did the trick, and the upgraded evaluation process was implemented during the current fiscal year.

I could share many more true stories of successful board chair-CEO collaboration, but the reader can easily see what board-savvy CEOs well know: investing in the development of a rock-solid board chair-CEO working relationship can yield powerful organizational dividends. In fact, I would suggest that one of the preeminent priorities of a truly board-savvy CEO is to transform her board chair into a strong governing partner, a reliable ally, and when needed, an ardent change champion. The board chair makes an especially important partner for the CEO not only because of her formal authority as "CEO" of the governing board, but also because board chairs are often major actors who wield tremendous influence in their communities, including in the profession or industry an association represents. I've seen board-savvy CEOs successfully employ five major strategies in building close and productive working relationships with their board chair:

1. Reach agreement with the board chair on the fundamental division of labor with the CEO.

2. Get to know the board chair really well.

3. Actively help the board chair succeed in her formal governing role.

4. Actively assist the board chair in having a richer, more satisfying experience beyond her formal leadership role.

5. And never miss an opportunity to provide the board chair with ego satisfaction, often in little but important ways.

"I'm not sure why you're talking about CEOs reaching agreement with their board chairs on the division of labor. Isn't it pretty obvious?" My response to this question, which came up last week in a nonprofit CEO seminar I was conducting, was an emphatic "Yes and no." Yes, it's true that the board chair is the formal leader of board deliberations, and normally organizational bylaws specify that he has the authority to appoint the chairs and members of the board's standing committees and ad hoc task forces and committees and to refer matters to the appropriate committee. But when you think about it, even that seemingly clear responsibility must be shared with the CEO for the simple reason that board chairs, being part-time volunteers for the most part, can't possibly play their board leader role alone. Active collaboration with, and strong support from, the CEO is essential for their success. And in the realm of external relations, both the board chair and CEO are commonly viewed as major actors, so they'd better pay some attention to coordination and division of labor or they'll be stumbling all over each other. So every board-savvy CEO I've ever worked with has made a point of sitting down with a new board chair to discuss in detail how they'll be working together.

Board-savvy CEOs who excel at partnering with their board chair always, in my experience, make a concerted effort to get to know their preeminent partner in-depth as quickly as they can, often starting with the resources that the board chair brings to her leadership role, including skills, expertise, knowledge, external connections, and reputation, to name some of the more important attributes. This is especially important in enlisting the board chair to provide leadership beyond merely chairing board meetings, since it would obviously be counterproductive to call on the board chair for leadership he isn't capable of providing. For example, a few years ago I worked with a board chair — a labor leader — who was a virtuoso at behind-the-scenes negotiation but terribly ineffectual as a public speaker — with his uninspiring monotone delivery and tendency to stumble over words. His board-savvy CEO knew enough to call on him as a partner in negotiating privately with key stakeholders like the county executive, but to avoid having him represent the nonprofit as a speaker in key forums like the monthly chamber of commerce luncheon or on radio talk shows.

Another way of knowing the board chair is to understand his preferred style of communicating. One of the less board-savvy CEOs I've ever worked with taught me a lesson about the price of failing to pay attention to his board chair's style a few years ago. The CEO, a college president, was finding it extremely frustrating trying to work with his relatively new board chair, an extraordinarily successful entrepreneur who had built a highly profitable company from scratch over the past quarter century, without the help of a college degree. Over and over again, the president would send his chair a well-crafted briefing paper on an issue coming up at the next board meeting, explaining why he was taking a particular position, only to receive no response at all. Charged with the responsibility to find out what was going on, I scheduled lunch with the chair, who shared with me how puzzled he was that the president was continually sending him long issue papers. He explained that he was actually pretty offended since anyone who took the trouble to get to know him would understand that he infinitely preferred a face-to-face sit-down over having to wade through a briefing paper. By the way, the problem did get worked out — by the president's changing his style and meeting for lunch once a week with his board chair to go over major issues deserving the chair's attention.

Really board-savvy CEOs make an effort to understand their new chair's professional aspirations and special interests, since, as I'll discuss later, one important way to strengthen the working relationship with the chair is to help her have a richer, more rewarding experience that goes beyond the formal board chair role. For example, the CEO of a public transit authority learned that his board chair was passionate about community and economic development issues and hoped that his leadership of the transit authority might earn him a seat at the community development table. And on a more personal note, the board chair of a children's services nonprofit confided to her CEO that she hoped that her leadership role would help her become more comfortable and skilled at public speaking, which she considered her most limiting professional weakness.

Almost all board chairs in the nonprofit and public sectors are unpaid volunteers, so truly board-savvy CEOs are always on the lookout for nonmonetary compensation that will not only reward the board chair for her service but will also help to cement the board chair-CEO working relationship. The most obvious is for the CEO to go out of his way to ensure that the chair succeeds in her formal governing role. For example, the president and CEO of a state professional association without fail spends at least an hour on the phone with his board chair before every meeting of the board's governance committee, which the chair heads, going over the agenda point by point, answering any questions the chair might have, thereby making sure the chair is well prepared to lead discussion.

The president of a community college whose board participates in an annual daylong strategic planning work session not only always makes sure that her board chair plays a leading role in developing the agenda, she also prepares opening remarks for the chair to deliver and ensures that her chair is assigned to the breakout groups in which she is most interested. And in the external affairs arena, the board-savvy superintendent of an urban school district provides meticulous support for his board chair's speaking engagements on behalf of the district, not only making sure the chair is armed with talking points and visual aids but even providing an opportunity to rehearse whenever the chair thinks it will help.

In my experience, many less board-savvy CEOs can easily miss the opportunity to cement the relationship with their board chair by helping her enrich her professional experience beyond the strict boundaries of her formal governing role. This is an important way the CEO can say, through concrete action, "I really do care about the quality of your experience, and I'll do what I can to make it more interesting and rewarding, beyond helping you succeed in your governing role." Don't doubt for a minute that such attentiveness can be a powerful relationship builder. Earlier I mentioned the example of a public transit board chair who was passionately interested in the area of community and economic development. As it happened, when the CEO was asked to fill a vacant seat on the board of the county economic development committee, he recommended that, instead, his board chair represent the authority on the commission board. When I was discussing this with the board chair a couple of months later, he made clear that he deeply appreciated his CEO's consideration, telling me that he was "bowled over" by the CEO's gesture.

And a tremendously board-savvy superintendent I was working with, knowing that her board chair was very interested in climbing the volunteer ladder in the state school boards association and eventually in the national association, went way out of her way to help her chair realize this professional vision. For one thing, she spent a half day with her chair one Saturday, helping her map out a strategy for rising through the volunteer ranks, including volunteering to serve on ad hoc committees and task forces. The superintendent even put together a proposal for a workshop that she and her board chair would present at the next state association conference, highlighting the governance improvements that had been implemented on the chair's watch. Not only was her chair touched by the superintendent's caring so deeply about her professional aspirations, the opportunity to work closely together in planning and presenting the workshop further solidified the relationship.

Board chairs are typically blessed with robust egos; that's one of the reasons they've become their boards' leaders. Board-savvy CEOs know that a fairly simple, inexpensive way to strengthen their relationship with the chair is to capitalize on opportunities to provide the chair with ego satisfaction. I've already talked about the big ways — such as making sure the chair succeeds in carrying out her formal governing role — but there are myriad smaller, less elaborate ways that CEOs can attend to their chair's ego needs if they're board savvy enough to pay attention. To take some common examples: inviting the board chair to sit in on a meeting with the local paper's editorial board or to participate in a radio talk show; recognizing the chair for her service in one of your nonprofit's publications; and making sure the chair keynotes the annual staff convocation.

I'll bring this discussion to a close by pointing out that failing to attend to the normal ego needs of the board chair can cost an un-board-savvy CEO dearly. Several years ago, I worked with the board chair and CEO of a large health services nonprofit that had successfully merged with a sister organization. The board chair had played a leading role in what turned out to be a grueling negotiation process that culminated in the merger, taking countless hours away from his legal practice over a period of six months. On one of my visits not long after the merger's implementation, I walked into the nonprofit's conference room for a meeting with the board chair and found him fuming. Asking what was wrong, I was handed the front page of the local paper, with a feature article on the merger. "Read this," he said. Puzzled that he wasn't more pleased at the front-page coverage, I read through the article. The CEO was quoted several times. Guess who wasn't quoted at all? Guess who hadn't even been invited to sit in on the meeting with the reporter who wrote the article? Guess who was still miffed weeks later? This is a perfect example of un-board-savviness at work. The sad thing is that if the CEO had been paying attention, making sure the board chair was mentioned prominently in the article would have been easy to accomplish.

EFFECTIVE BOARD EVALUATION OF CEO PERFORMANCE

I was fortunate to have the opportunity to sit in on a fascinating, highly productive work session around three weeks ago that lasted a little over three hours. The governance committee of the board of a professional association was conducting the end-of-year evaluation of its fairly new president and CEO's performance. The first hour of the session was devoted to discussing the CEO's performance in terms of association-wide outcome targets that had been established for the year just ended in the annual operational planning/budget process. The discussion focused on such outcome measures as membership numbers, attendance at the annual conference and at various educational programs that had been presented during the year, the profitability of income-generating programs such as the annual conference, overall revenue growth, and the like. Making and exceeding targets was noted, but most of the discussion centered on targets that were not met. By the way, the president had prepared for the session by putting together an explanation for the shortfalls in performance that she knew would be highlighted.

The final two-thirds of the session were devoted to the president's CEO-centric outcome targets that had been negotiated with the governance committee a little more than a year ago. These targeted outcomes, which were explicitly tied to the president's chief executive leadership priorities and which involved significant presidential time, fell into four main leadership categories:

1. *Association strategic growth* —The president had committed to the full implementation of a strategy to grow the association's membership and participation in educational programs by specific percentages in selected countries outside the US.

2. *External/member relations* —The president had committed to im-

proving the association's image among its members as measured by a member survey that had recently been administered.

3. *Internal management* —The president had committed to significantly upgrading the association's financial management capacity, including hiring a well-qualified chief financial officer and completing a major overhaul of the accounting system.

4. *Board of directors' support* —The president had committed to working closely with the governance committee in developing and implementing a comprehensive program to strengthen board member governing knowledge and skills, including a completely redesigned process for orienting new board members.

The president had also prepared for the latter segment of the evaluation session by documenting progress in achieving her CEO-centric targets and explaining any performance problems she had encountered. What hit me in the face as I observed this lively session was how substantive the discussion was from beginning to end. By focusing on two tiers of outcomes, the board's governance committee got to the heart of the president's performance and was able to deal with truly important performance issues, such as an actual decline in attendance at the annual conference. Three further steps were taken to complete the evaluation process after this three-hour meeting. First, the governance committee briefed the full board on the evaluation results and solicited board members' feedback. Second, the governance committee finalized its evaluation and reviewed it with the president. And third, the governance committee set the president's compensation for the coming year. The ultimate bottom line? Agreement between the board and its CEO on performance issues that she needed to address over the coming year.

Board-savvy CEOs do their utmost to make sure that a substantive, meaningful process for the board to evaluate their performance, like the one I've just described, is designed and fully implemented. Not only do they want a process that focuses on outcomes and hence protects the best interests of the whole organization, the board, and the CEO, they also recognize that a well-designed and executed evaluation process is a major tool for keeping the board-CEO working relationship healthy. The example of a meaningful process that I've just described is dramatically different from the kinds of mechanistic, ritualistic, and pseudoscientific "instruments" that I've seen many nonprofit and public organizations employ. I can't tell you how many questionnaires I've come across that boards have used to "scientifically" measure CEO performance in major functional areas. For example, board members are asked to assess how effective the CEO is in representing her nonprofit in the external world or in providing the board with support, or in filling top positions — often on a scale of one to five. Being disconnected from concrete targeted outcomes, these patently subjective opinion surveys obviously widely miss the mark and can end up doing more harm than good.

I haven't done any research to determine why board evaluation of CEO performance is often not done at all or done in a highly subjective fashion that misses the point. My guess is that three major factors are at work: board member awkwardness about evaluating a CEO who is often a peer or even a professional superior; board members' lack of knowledge and expertise in this area; and reluctance to commit more time than it takes to fill out a mechanistic survey instrument. Whatever the reasons many nonprofit leaders don't, board-savvy CEOs make putting a meaningful evaluation process into practice a high priority.

LOTS OF INFORMAL INTERACTION

I'll close with a very brief look at informal interaction as a relationship-building tool. A couple of hours before every quarterly board meeting, the board, CEO and executive team of a regional economic development corporation get together for an informal lunch. There's no formal agenda; the point isn't to prepare for the upcoming meeting. Instead, board and staff members sit together at five-person round tables. (Pre-assigning seats ensures a mix of board and staff members at each table.) The only formal guidelines are that board business not be discussed at the tables and that participants get to know each other better. An interesting twist is that participants are requested to take another look before every quarterly pre-board meeting lunch at the extensive board and executive team member biographical sketches, including personal information such as kids' names and ages, that are maintained, and regularly updated, in a special section of the corporation's Web site. In practice, this simple technique has proved to be an effective conversation booster. Other nonprofits I've worked with have brought board and staff members together at holiday parties and summer picnics — often with their families — and, as I've mentioned earlier, many board-savvy CEOs make a point of regularly sitting down over breakfast or lunch with individual board members.

Informal board-staff interaction might appear to be a somewhat frivolous topic, at least by comparison with what's come before in this last chapter, but board-savvy CEOs know that such interaction breeds familiarity, which tends to be a glue that more strongly binds relationships. To be sure, it's not a major-league partnership-building strategy, but enough finer touches like the quarterly lunch I described above can make a difference, so my counsel to CEOs is to capitalize on opportunities for informal interaction, as an important means of promoting intimacy and narrowing emotional distance — in other words, of humanizing and deepening professional relationships. Not only does it facilitate cooperation and collaboration, it creates a line of credit that can be drawn on when tackling the kind of complex, high-stakes, tension-inducing issues that are not only common at the top of an organization but that can seriously tax the most solid relationships.

ABOUT THE AUTHOR

President and CEO of Doug Eadie & Company, Doug Eadie has for the past quarter century provided consulting assistance to more than 500 nonprofit and public organizations, helping them build rock-solid board-CEO partnerships and take command of their own change. Before founding his consulting firm, Doug served as a Peace Corps teacher for three years in Addis Ababa, Ethiopia, and held a number of senior executive positions in the nonprofit and public sectors. Doug's twenty books include four in addition to *The Board-Savvy CEO* from Governance Edge Publishing: *Leading Out-of-the-Box Change* (2012); *The Blind Visionary* (with Virginia Jacko, 2010); *Building a Rock-Solid Partnership With Your Board* (2008); and *Meeting the Governing Challenge* (2007). Doug is also the author of more than one hundred articles that have appeared in such publications as *Associations Now* (American Society of Association Executives), *Forum* (Association Forum of Chicagoland), *Nonprofit World* (Society for Nonprofits), and the *Journal of Nonprofit Education and Leadership*. A Phi Beta Kappa graduate of the University of Illinois at Urbana-Champaign, Doug was awarded the master of science in management degree from Case Western Reserve University's Weatherhead School of Management. He and his wife, Barbara Krai, reside in Tampa Bay, Florida.

CPSIA information can be obtained
at www.ICGtesting.com
Printed in the USA
BVHW08s0158110818
524184BV00002B/77/P

9 780979 889493